An Alpine Thi~~n~~

A jaunt through the French mountains

by an old bloke on an even older bike

Noel Whittall

Noel W
Dec 2016

Propagator Press

This book is published by Propagator Press

Propagator Press
38 Parkside Road
Leeds
LS6 4NB

ISBN 978-1-908037-26-8

Designed by Propagator Press
Printed in Great Britain

Contents

Acknowledgements

I am grateful to the countless vintage motorcycle enthusiasts from whom I have accumulated the lore required to keep an old bike running under varied conditions. However, my own bodges and dodges would be useless without the sound engineering service provided by Ian Jennings during the preparation stages. There is no-one better!

A ferry-missing disaster at the start of my June ride through the Benelux countries was averted by rapid and freely-given retrieval service from fellow VMCC member Bob McConnell, to whom I will be forever grateful. I just caught the boat at Hull and the ride turned out to be a good training exercise for the Alps.

Rosita Whittall proof-read the first draft and I appreciated her encouragement and that of my son Matthew. However, it is a foolish author who depends of the praise of family, so I am extra grateful to Stan Sharp of Propagator Press who had the faith to take on this second book about *H* and me.

Simon Smith and the Amazing Dancing Bear (1967) by Randy Newman, ©Warner/Chappell Music

Introduction

The fuel is on. The toe of my right boot flicks up the half-compression lever on the side of the engine, which like the rest of the bike is going on for a hundred years old.

I set the throttle lever one-quarter open and the air lever to three-quarters, then swing the kick-starter. The engine fires as usual and I immediately knock the half-compression lever downwards, to the 'run' position. The exhaust note of the old Triumph sharpens at once and I fine-adjust the throttle and air levers to give the steady slow tick over that I know so well. I have gone through this routine hundreds of times, but this one is different. I am not just starting out on a run, it is the start of a special trip. The plan is that my Triumph – 'H' to her friends – will carry me over all the highest mountain passes in France. We are going to tackle the *Route Des Grandes Alpes*!

Yes, this is a book about riding an ancient motorbike, but it is also about having a small adventure, and small adventures are the seasoning in the stew of life. I do not delude myself that reading this will inspire anyone else to follow me over the mountains on a boneshaker, but I hope it will make some readers recall slightly strange things about which they have thought, *'I'd love to do that someday'* – and set about doing them ... soon! Even better ... now!

I love riding very old motorcycles and I like mountains very much. I also have a distant interest in the Tour de France cycle race and admire the stamina of the competitors as they tackle climb after climb. I know I could not hope to do the same pedal pushing, but it had made me wonder how my early belt-driven motorcycle would cope with a succession of genuine Alpine passes. There was one obvious way to find out ...

It is generally accepted that the Route Des Grandes Alpes starts on the south shore of Lake Geneva at the genteel spa town of Thonon-les-Bains and continues through the mountains to the Mediterranean Sea at Menton. As the crow flies, it is about 200 miles, but if any crows were involved in route plotting when the project was conceived back in the 1900s , they must have been on foot and smashed out of their brains. The Route is tortuous, linking mountain passes one after another. As soon as one is conquered you are down through the high pastures, into a gorge, along a valley, maybe through a small town, and then climbing out above the tree-line again. A century ago, it was devised as a bold idea to generate income in the highest and most remote parts of mainland France by encouraging touring, first by bicycle and then by motor. It is fair to say that it has been successful, although nowadays much of the success can be attributed to the cycling, thanks to TV coverage of those Tour de France pelotons labouring up the major cols.

I had been vaguely aware of the Route's existence for many years, but it was not until I read a brief feature in a contemporary motorcycle magazine that I began to think about having a go at it. I don't remember which magazine it was, but the message I retained was to the effect that 'if you have a large modern motorcycle with plenty of power, you should be OK'. It is, then, hard to explain why I immediately began to contemplate tackling it on an ancient motorcycle with very little power indeed – my 1918 Triumph Model H – but those who know me may not be too surprised.

Noel Whittall May 2013

Chapter 1
Meet *H*

The Machine

H is a single-cylinder Triumph motorcycle which was
supplied to the War Department for despatch rider duty. The
design was introduced in 1915 and mine was built in 1918. I
acquired her ten or so years ago and since then we have come to an
excellent working agreement: she delivers loyal service and in
return I treat her as an elderly aunt who is still pretty game, but
needs occasional looking after. The arrangement suits us both.
Three or four years ago we rode from my home in Leeds to John
o' Groats, then down to Land's End and back home again, so we
know each other quite well.

Let's get the tedious technical details out of the way quickly.
Feel free to skip this bit if you would just like to get on with the
trip.

H – just waiting for a new adventure

The Engine

At the heart of *H* is a motor with a single cast-iron cylinder mounted on an aluminium crankcase. It is classed as 4HP. The cylinder capacity is 550cc – think of it as near enough an Imperial pint – and it is swept by a cast-iron piston. The compression ratio is only about 4.5:1. The piston, by courtesy of the crank-pin to which it is connected, turns a hefty pair of iron flywheels.

It is a four-stroke side-valve engine, the valve stems, springs and tappets being fully exposed on the right-hand side. If you feel so disposed, you can watch the whole lot going up and down when the motor is running. At tick-over the effect can be quite mesmeric. When *H* was originally made, there was still much to be learned about the steel alloy best suited for these valves. They were the weakest point of all early motorcycles and it was quite common for them to break. However, *H* is now fitted with valves adapted from a type intended for duty in diesel Ford Transits and they have an excellent resistance to pain.

The cylinder barrel, head and combustion chamber are combined in one iron casting, together with the inlet and exhaust ports. It is quite a complicated lump of metal. The piston, which goes up and down within this lot, is also cast iron, which to the modern motorcyclist may seem an eccentric choice, yet it works very well because when it gets hot it expands at about the same rate as the barrel, so piston seizures are rare. This is a motor which revs slowly, so the weight of cast iron is a minor consideration: it spends most of its working life running between 1,000 and 2,000 rpm. Tick over can be as low as 120 rpm.

It can be argued that such an engine is primitive, and by current standards it is. It could do with a few more cooling fins, as it runs rather hot. However, it is extremely well built from high-quality materials and seems prepared to provide reliable power almost indefinitely.

Lubrication is simple. A syringe-type pump is mounted in the oil compartment of the tank and linked directly to the crankcase. It is up to the rider to remember this and give it a squirt every so often. The handbooks suggest one full stroke of the pump every 10 miles, which at normal cruising speeds equates to every twenty minutes. I prefer to give a half-stroke every 10 minutes because I have a short memory. Regardless of how much oil is pumped, it is either burned or leaks out. This is very accurately called the *total-loss* system.

Transmission

The engine drives by chain to a three-speed gearbox, then to the rear wheel through a flexible vee-belt. The gears are selected with a hand lever to the right of the fuel tank. Push down for first gear, then back up through neutral to second and third. The clutch lever is on the left handlebar. It is light enough to be operated with one finger.

In the early days of motorcycling the vee-belts were made from leather, treated with various types of patent dressing to maintain flexibility. By the time *H* was made, moulded rubber-and-canvas had replaced leather. Both these types of belt worked very well when new, but joining their ends together was always a problem and a weak point. They eventually came to be superseded by belting made of many overlapping links of rubberised fabric. These are generally referred to as *Brammer* type, and that is what I use. They work well, but need knowing. They need to be clean, dry and at just the correct tension to grip reliably – not a problem on a run round the parish, but easier said than done on a long tour. The tension is affected to some extent by temperature and the grip is influenced by the presence of water and/or oil. Rain, leaky gearbox and freezing mountain tops ahead. Hmmm.

Fuel system

Petrol. I use the most expensive because at the time of writing it is likely to contain less ethanol than the cheap grades and at about 100mpg, fuel for *H* is not a major expense. *H* would be happy burning almost any flammable liquid, but the wretched ethanol which is steadily (and in my opinion, stupidly) imposed upon us, encourages rust within the tank and attacks the paint on the outside, given half a chance. Therefore, I try to avoid it.

The fuel runs by gravity from the tank (approx 1.1/2 gallons) to Triumph's own carburettor. I have heard these described as crude but I think 'displaying glorious simplicity' suits them better. There are two identical cylindrical slides, the rear one governing the air intake and the front, the fuel mixture. Between them is the jet, up through which fuel is drawn by the air rushing across it in its eagerness to enter the cylinder. It is up to the rider to judge how much air to give, according to the conditions of the moment. The slides are controlled from a double lever on the right of the handlebars – twist grip throttles were not common on British bikes until the late 1920s.

Ignition

H came with a Lucas magneto to provide the sparks, but I prefer the Bosch variety and have fitted one manufactured in 1912. So far it has given flawless service and required no attention during the period of this book. The timing of the spark can be adjusted from a lever on the left of the handlebars. Broadly speaking, the spark should be advanced as the engine speeds up and retarded for starting and slow-running.

Braking

All the controls work smoothly and in spite of initially being suspicious of *H*'s quaint and spindly appearance, riders of modern motorcycles have little difficulty in adapting to her on clear roads when they have accepted my offer to 'give her a try'. However, this can easily lead to over confidence because sooner or later they will discover that my supplementary instruction to *'Ride as if there are no brakes because that way you will avoid disappointment'* is sound advice indeed. *H*'s brakes can kindly be described as 'slight' at the best of times and in heavy rain they depart altogether.

A foot pedal on the left works the rear brake. This is simply a wedging block which presses into the same rim as the drive-belt. When all is clean and dry, this has been known to lock the wheel, but not for long and you can never bank on it. The front brake is influenced via a puny lever on the end of the right handlebar. It is connected to a stirrup brake on the front rim, of a pattern normally found on old-time vicars' bicycles. In an emergency this generates a squeaking noise but has no effect on the process of deceleration. Perversely, *H*'s engine is her most dependable aid to slowing down and/or controlling rate of descent. Simply closing the throttle helps a lot, but the real trick is to use a lever at the end of the left handlebar which is the 'valve lifter'. Using this stops the exhaust valve from seating, so the engine doesn't fire and simply turns into a rather inefficient air pump which absorbs lots of energy and delivers little in return. Of course, it won't make an emergency stop for you, but it does prevent the bike from running away on a long descent – very handy in the mountains as I was frequently to prove.

All the rest

The frame is clearly derived from bicycles of the period, just beefed-up a bit to deal with the extra stress of a motor. Springing is modest – being a single one at the front allowing the forks to move back and forth, rather than up and down. This copes with moderate bumps rather better than appearance suggests. The saddle springs also do a surprisingly good job.

The wheels are the size and type a hefty bicycle may have used. They take old-fashioned beaded-edge tyres of 2.1/2in section which are best run at above 40psi (2.5Bar) to be sure they are persuaded not to 'creep' on the rims. There is a lot more about these tyres in Chapter 18, but this is all you really need to know.

Mudguarding is excellent and the rear carrier is stout and well-designed. The rear stand is good, but the bike has to be lifted up onto it. This becomes a tedious effort on any journey with frequent stops. The front stand is brought into play only for tyre changing at that end. There is no prop stand as they don't seem to have been invented in time.

So there is *H* as she is today. Various parts have been repaired and replaced during her 95 years, but I don't think her first owner would have any difficulty in identifying her. Although, come to think of it, he may be a bit mystified by the twenty pence piece I soldered on to reinforce the housing round the half-compression lever.

Chapter 2

Getting there

*'I may go out tomorrow if I can borrow a coat to wear
Oh I'll go out in style with my sassy smile and a dancing
bear'*

A week into September: my VW Caddy Maxi van is humming down the Autoroute, cruise control set somewhere around 130kph, a pile of Euros on hand to pay the ransoms at the toll booths, *H* safely tied down in the back and a CD of 60's hits playing away in the dashboard. I have very poor taste in music and negligible talent for holding a tune in my head, but when one manages to get there it really does stick. When *H* and I did the John o' Groats to Land's End thing a couple or so years ago, it was the old folk song *Hunting the Wren* which provided the musical accompaniment. I would find myself singing it anywhere and everywhere en route: on the long boring straights, through the twisty bits and even in moments of vehicular crisis. This time it would be *Simon Smith and the Amazing Dancing Bear* which worked its way into my skull and stayed there over the passes in the Route des Grandes Alpes. The Harry Nilssen version, although Alan Price would have done just as well.

Why am I in the van and not riding *H*? Sheer practicality, I'm afraid. I had set out to ride to the South of France at Jubilee time in June. On a moist morning *H* and I rode to Hull, took the ferry to Rotterdam and aimed generally south. However, after a couple of weeks paddling around the Benelux countries in the rain and with a further week of vigorous Atlantic depressions forecast to batter my planned route south from Verdun, I metaphorically chucked in the towel (which was soaking anyway) and rode home via

Zeebrugge and Hull. It even rained all the way from Hull back to Leeds. I would try again later.

Now, a couple of months later, I am almost floating, not on water but through the French air. The clear blue of the morning has become flecked with white cumulus. Each cloud marks a thermal, a column of rising air, and often I can see a buzzard using that lift for a free ride, gaining altitude without effort. There is little traffic and I speed smoothly through the flat agricultural hectares around Rheims, an area of vast fields and monstrous tractors. Then past Troyes and Chaumont. Soon enough Dijon is on the signboards and I have left Champagne for the undulations of Burgundy. It is a crime to swallow up this magnificent historic countryside with speed, but today I am hungry for distance. I need to get to the Alps! Distant skies become hazy with dust as the day ages. Vineyards and chateaux rule and punctuate the hillsides of the Côte d'Or. We whistle past Beaune, aiming towards Lyon but turning off left for Bourg-en-Bresse, still on the Péage, with the mountains of the Jura sunlit to the east and Geneva on the signboards.

Hours and kilometres pass effortlessly on the smooth uncrowded road. I am always happy to approach mountain ranges by road, watching them gradually define themselves and occupy more and more of the space between earth and sky. It gives me a feeling of excited anticipation, regardless of whether I have been among the same mountains previously. It is rather like a grand version of the extended drum-roll at the beginning of the overture at a panto when I was eight or nine. Arrival by air simply doesn't do it. So I drive on, buoyed up not only by the prospect of the approaching Alps, but also by frequent plays of *The Amazing Dancing Bear* and occasional wine gums.

Then I enter the stretch of Autoroute running along the side of the Val St-Julien; it must be one of the most spectacular examples of highway engineering imaginable. Great two-level concrete viaducts are hung on the mountainside, always curving sufficiently to display themselves to either direction. We are still in France, within whose borders we will remain for the entire journey, whether in van or on the motorcycle. It is important to pay attention to navigation as Geneva approaches, because it is easy to make a mistake and stray into Switzerland, where you are required to pay for a year's use of their motorways, even if all you want to do is get off them at the earliest opportunity. No, it didn't happen to me, but I know a few who have been so caught.

Paragliders dot the late-afternoon sky like Scottish midges as the bulk of Mont Salève comes into view. I am not the only one having a good day. Soon after passing below the wires of the Salève cable-car, I turn the van towards Annemasse and on along the back roads towards Thonon-les-Bains, in the middle of the south bank of Lake Geneva – *Lac Léman*, as I must remember to call it from now on. I am on the lookout for any friendly small hotel, where I can not only stay the night, but also leave the van for a week or two while *H* and I go off over the mountains. I try a couple, but the response is the same at each: 'Sorry, Monsieur, but we are full – marriage!'

Apparently the wedding season is in full swing this September in France. I should have been prepared for this because at my overnight stop near Dunkirk, the night before, I had been unable to visit my usual restaurant because it was packed with wedding carousers. And come to think of it, I had later followed an implausibly shiny Citröen 2CV with white satin bows on its door-handles as it wallowed its way towards Thonon. The signs were all there ...

I went on into the central hotel area of the town and found parking to be on the impossible side of difficult. The prospects of leaving the van there for an indeterminate stay were remote anyway, so I drove on, stopping briefly at the only shop where I could park – a supermarket. I thought I might find a guide to the *Route* in their quite-extensive book section, but there was not a hint.

Eventually I found myself back in Annemasse, which somehow manages to give off an air of being Geneva's impoverished half-sister. A sign directed me to 'Hotel Premier Classe', one of a chain of budget hotels, several of which I have used in the past. This particular example was the Camp Bastion version. Rarely have I spent a night in a building which felt quite so much like a barracks or correctional institution. But, hey, it's only one night and, at less than 50 Euros with a satisfactory breakfast thrown in, I was not being robbed. Dinner was a different matter: the only place within walking distance was a vast timber shed with an extreme-sports theme. I had to force a path through a horde of enthusiastic smokers to get in and soon spotted that the dress code was based upon *The Only Way is Essex*. The only extreme things here were fake tans and eyelashes! A burger joint is a burger joint, no matter how you dress it up. And a burger is only a burger even if the menu insists on calling it a 'Vingt-quatre Heures du Mans', or something equally incongruous. I had read that French youth had embraced the burger culture, but didn't imagine that they could have been brainwashed to this extent. By any burger standards the food was average, yet the place was heaving. I could have done better for half the price in Dewsbury or Halifax.

I set off next morning with a slightly revised plan: rather than seeking a base in Thonon, I would drive along the start of the Route and search for a hotel a short distance along it, in the winter sports areas around Morzine. It turned out to be a brilliant plan.

Additional guidance for first-timers on French Autoroutes

In the event that my example may tempt motorcyclists onto the generally excellent Autoroute system for the first time, these notes are offered to help ease your progress. Believe me, they are the fruit of experience.

Undoubtedly your background research will have prepared you for the need to have adequate cash, or better still, a Euro cashcard, in an outside pocket to get you through the tolls without the ritual undressing, burrowing and glove-dropping at the head of that ever-increasing queue which characterises British newcomers. However, that research may not have given you the low-down on how to conduct yourself at the Autoroute minor rest areas.

These lesser parking areas have no fuel station or shop and are unattended, but do offer 24-hour toilet facilities, a blessing sadly missing from our own Motorways. Imagine the scene: you park the bike and stride confidently past a few picnickers to the privy block. There is a cubicle free. Joy! But it soon turns to sorrow when you observe that some toe-rag has stolen the bowl. Have no dismay. You are simply experiencing your first encounter with the *scooter* lavatory, so named because its use requires the adoption of the pose of someone with no visible means of support guiding a Lambretta against a stiff headwind.

The best advice at this stage is to withdraw for a moment or two and take stock of your situation. Sharp observation is paramount! You will notice the two raised footplates on the floor and the ominous hole nearby, so can easily deduce the orientation required for action. Before even thinking of taking up Position 1, you need to be able to answer the following questions: 'Does the door open inwards or out? Is there a hook on the door for your jacket? Are there grab handles? Is there paper within reach?' It is also well to remember that during the process of taking up the required crouch almost anything can and will be expelled from an unguarded trousers' pocket. There are few less-appealing ways of starting a holiday than having to rummage for valuables in the unspeakable depths of an un-flushed scooter so transfer your wallet / keys / passport to the jacket for which, hopefully, there will be a hook on the door. This is all elementary stuff but overlook it at your peril. For example, if the door opens inwards, try and spot whether there is an area of high ground within the cubicle to which you may retreat during the flush cycle if need be. Flushing can be spectacularly vigorous and often induces a flash flood – no fun at all if your escape route is blocked by an inward-opening door.

Motorcycle clothing is generally fairly well suited to purpose. Unfortunately that purpose does not extend to facile use of scooter toilets. Consider the case of one-piece leathers: once you have got them down around your knees, the essential need to keep the sleeves off the ground and clear of the action will occupy at least one hand fully. The other hand is needed to maintain a death-grip on a grab-handle (only the young, the desperate and accomplished international gymnasts should even *think* of tackling a *handle-less* scooter). The death-grip is recommended because within half a minute or so the compressed leathers will constrict the flow of blood to the legs to the extent that retaining balance is no longer guaranteed. Also, in the absence of a third hand, there is an inevitability that sooner or later you are you going to have to release either suit or handle or, if the roll of paper is not fortuitously located, both. A time for careful planning and stealthy action with precise control. A two-piece suit is only slightly less of a challenge and heaven help you if braces are involved.

In fact, these scooter toilets are very good and, on an unattended site, far more hygienic than many of the unspeakable alternatives I have encountered. The stainless steel scooters by the Autoroutes are a capital introduction to the porcelain, terra-cotta and cement variations you may well encounter on travels in France. It's a world rich in adventure and discovery out there. Bonne chance mes amis!

It is not only motorcycle clothing that requires careful management in scooter toilets; they have frequently proved themselves to be the natural enemy of the flip-flop.

Chapter 3

Getting going

I had imagined that the start of the Route des Grandes Alpes would be generously signposted in Thonon-les-Bains. I visualised a garlanded arch and lots of arrows. I thought the tourist authorities would have been keen to make something of it, but if they did, I missed it.

Still raring to go

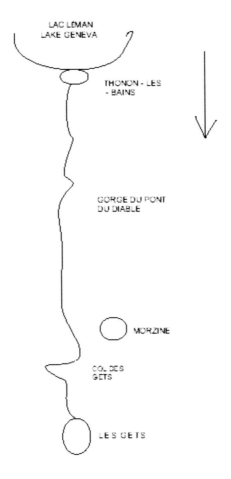

On Sunday morning, September 9, with *H* still strapped in the back of the van, I drove into the town, once around the centre and out up the hillside of the Geneva basin, following the directions to Morzine. One more roundabout and there, just at the start of a dark ravine, is a *Route des Grandes Alpes* board. It was the first clear evidence that I was indeed in the right area. Uplifted, with confidence restored, I pressed on. This is the *Gorge du Diable* – the Devil's Gorge – and it lets you know that you are in the mountains. I reckoned that *H* would be able to climb it OK, but thought she would probably need quite a lot of second-gear work. Eventually, I got to Morzine, a town I have spent some time in during earlier incarnations as paraglider pilot and skier. It is excellent for both those activities, but not so good if long-term parking is required. I eventually untangled the van from the traffic and made for Les Gets (pronounce it *Lay Jay* and you won't be far off) a smaller town just a few kilometres further up the mountainside, at the top of the Col des Gets. Here I found just the sort of hotel I had been searching for, in the form of La Bonne Franquette, where Madame Anthonioz provided a warm welcome, a pleasant room and limitless free parking for the van.

By now it was mid-morning and I had no excuse for not getting on the bike. The VW van was parked under a convenient tree, *H* was rolled out, fuelled up and it was showtime. I knew I would be dissatisfied if I did not complete the *whole* Route des Grandes Alpes, so I decided to ride down the gorge to Thonon - les-Bains and back again. It all went well; over the Devil's bridge, down past a group of white-water canoeists who waved vigorously as *H* chuffed past, on through town outskirts, over the level-crossing, to the very edge of Lac Léman. We stopped in a small park beside some fountains. The centre of Thonon on a Sunday morning is quiet almost to the point of extinction. We had to wait some time before a couple appeared and I was able to persuade them to take our photo. Of course, we posed outrageously.

Posing

Now that I really knew which way to go out of town, the return to Les Gets was simple. I paused at the roadside to take a photo of the first 'Route des Grandes Alpes' sign by the roadside, where I was soon joined by a German motorcyclist who was doing the same thing. That was to set a bit of a pattern for the rest of my journey. *H* was running beautifully and we motored up the shady gorge in fine style, again getting enthusiastic waves from groups of kayakers. She galloped up the steady incline and round the tight bends in top gear all the way – confounding my earlier impression that the middle one of her three gears would be needed for much of the climb. Sunlight streamed onto the cafe near the bridge, where we paused for a lunch-break. Sitting under a parasol, eating a fresh cheese-and-ham baguette and watching the traffic go by, passed another pleasant half-hour and I felt that I was at last travelling through a part of France where I could be really relaxed in spite of having chosen a fairly irrational mode of transport.

I got back to the hotel by mid-afternoon. The way the bike had pulled up the gorge was impressive, but it also brought home to me the amount of work the rear tyre had to perform. I was running on a rather old Dunlop which had already taken me from Land's End to John o' Groats and back again. I had reckoned it had enough life left in it to get me over an Alp or several, but now I was not so sure. The more I looked at it, the thinner the tread seemed. I imagined great gashes inflicted by stone-strewn tracks up the mountains. I had brought a newer tyre with me, an *Ensign*, manufactured by a Far Eastern company. I had thrown it into the van at the last minute, almost as an afterthought. It had done a few hundred miles on my other ancient Triumph. I recalled that when it was new, fitting it onto the rim had been an absolute swine of a task which had left me covered in sweat and exhausted of profanities. Should I now try and strap it to the bike somehow and carry it with me in case the Dunlop finally gave out, or should I ...? Images of wrestling to change a tyre in pouring rain on a mountainside entered my consciousness and after a few minutes I had talked myself into doing the sensible thing, in itself a rarity. I would change it now, in this nice level hotel car park.

Off with the belt, out with the wheel, off with the tyre and tube. It didn't take long. The replacement Ensign went into place easily – the time it had spent on the other bike had stretched it and formed it enough to make a huge difference. Pumping it up to working pressure with the bicycle-type pump I had on the bike took ages, but eventually everything was together again and I felt quite pleased with the whole day.

It was late afternoon; dinner in my hotel was at 7:30, so I did the obvious thing and strolled down to a hotel/bar nearby and sipped a beer while trying to unravel, with little success, the animated chat of several French holidaymakers seated nearby. Opposite, the pistes down which I had skied only a few winters ago were now just green flanks on the mountainside. Skiing is the only pleasure that my dodgy heart has deprived me of, but I have adjusted to that small loss and am content. This bar is a great place for feeling content. An almost non-stop column of motos flows past before me, slowing and as they negotiate a tight little roundabout followed by a descending right-hander which takes them away down a short gorge towards Taninges and Cluses. I have a great view. All the regular names – Ducati, BMW, Honda, Yamaha, Suzuki, Triumph are present – interspersed with relative rarities such as KTM and Aprilia. They are almost all sports models ridden by anonymous beings in full-crouch under dark-visored helmets and give the impression that the bikes demand constant restraint, like young bullterriers on short leads. They brake and change-down fussily for the roundabout, take the right-hander on neutral throttle and disappear into the gorge with echoing bellows of relief. Were they all aiming for the Mediterranean as I would be tomorrow, or were they just out for a local blast?

It had been a good prelude; the morning would bring the start of the real thing! I ambled off to dinner. It was excellent and needed half a page in my notebook. I am not going to reel off the menu here, as it is early in the book and the scope for getting tedious about good French cooking is limitless. I sought a translation for the hotel's name, *La Bonne Franquette*, and the nearest I could get was 'no problems'. Just so.

Today I had peeled the first layer off the mystery of the Route, but was still only playing about within range of my van and its comforting assemblage of tools and spares: tomorrow it would begin to get serious.

Approximate distance Les Gets – Thonon – Les Gets:

50miles/80km

Chapter 4

What is the Route des Grandes Alpes?

Well, on the map it is mainly *Route Départmentale 902*, or D902 for short, but of course there is a lot more to it than just that.

The first stirrings of the Route as a tourist itinerary started more than 100 years ago. The boom in cycling of the 1890s and the development of practical cars and motorcycles shortly afterwards gave people a mobility undreamed of earlier. Soon cyclists and adventurous motorists began to venture to parts of the Alps unserved by railways – boosting the very poor economy of the area. This became formalised by the Touring Club of France with the launching of the Route des Grandes Alpes in 1909. It linked the fashionable watering places of Thonon les Bains on Lake Geneva with Nice, on the Mediterranean.

This was really a map exercise – the officials of the Touring Club didn't set out immediately with shovels to create the Route, which already existed in one form or another. They did lots of planning and promotion which was to lead to the steady development of the Route over four or five decades; initially only the roads through the larger towns were paved, but by the 1950s most of it was tarmac. Much of it was based on military roads which had started as mule tracks, developed to service fortifications overlooking prime Alpine passes. Any power which could control a pass could also control the trade and extract taxes almost at will. The trade was large and valuable – not just local produce, but material from Africa and the Middle East, already shipped across the Mediterranean into ports such as Genoa and now making its way up into middle Europe. Naturally this proved attractive to despots with extravagant lifestyles to support, so for centuries the Alps tended to be a rugged battleground where the Houses of Savoy, Piedmont, Austro-Hungary and Tuscany, among others, settled their differences, often egged-on from Rome by the Papacy.

The Col de L'Iseran opened in 1937 after almost ten years of work. It was the highest point of the original Route and opened with great ceremony by Albert Lebrun, the Président de la Republic at the time. At 2770m (9087ft) it was for many years the highest motor pass in Europe, but has now been exceeded by the Col de la Bonette, which we will get to in Chapter 8. There are other paved roads which are higher, but I believe they are all dead ends.

The passes often seem to be clinging onto the contours of the mountain, but they are rarely very steep; long, yes, spectacular, yes, but certainly not as steep as the worst you may find in England. The kilometres to the top are usually marked with stones giving the average gradient percentage for the next section – typically 7% or 8%. This is done for the benefit of cyclists but I suspect it may demoralise as many as it encourages.

The figures I give for the heights of passes are generally taken from a Michelin map or the signboards on the cols. My advice would be to treat them with some suspicion as whenever I double-check I can come up with variations according to the sources consulted. It is probably simpler to accept that they are all bloody high and the views are wonderful.

Chapter 5
Les Gets to Val d'Isère

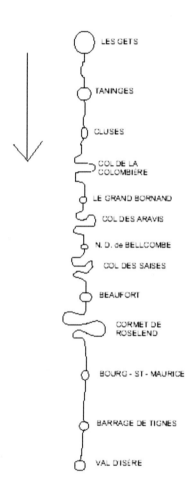

LES GETS

TANINGES

CLUSES

COL DE LA COLOMBIÈRE

LE GRAND BORNAND

COL DES ARAVIS

N. D. de BELLCOMBE

COL DES SAISES

BEAUFORT

CORMET DE ROSELEND

BOURG - ST - MAURICE

BARRAGE DE TIGNES

VAL D'ISÈRE

Monday 10 September

Here we go. I checked that the van was positioned in the hotel car park so that it would inconvenience no-one for a week or two – not really a problem in low-season – and set about my customary meticulous pre-ride routine. As usual there were a few gaps in it. *H* was extracted, the oil and fuel tanks topped-up, the tyres kicked in lieu of a pressure check and that was about it. The rear one, fitted the previous day, was not just as hard as I like but I had forgotten to bring my foot-pump and didn't fancy further effort with the weedy on-board equipment which is really only a bicycle hand-pump. I decided that it would get me to a garage with an air-line and hoped for the best. I do a lot of that.

I loaded the panniers onto the bike, decided that they were over-full and set about removing anything I was pretty sure I could do without. I was fairly strict with myself about this and a shirt, a comfy woolly, some extra socks and my iPad were consigned to the van. I was to regret this later, although the socks were no great loss.

Part of my rigorous planning programme back in England had taken into account the desirability of complying with French traffic laws, albeit in a fairly freestyle way. For as long as I can remember, the authorities have had an obsession with vehicle lighting. Years ago it was insistence on yellow bulbs, which meant that it was only renegade foreigners who could actually see where they were going on unlit roads after dark. Then there were purges on incorrect angles of dip and tales of distraught Brits being turned back at Calais for minor infringements. As *H* is not over-blessed in the lighting department (not blessed at all, in fact) and I knew that my Alpine route would involve several tunnels where lights are mandatory, I had taken the precaution of buying a rather good modern bicycle headlamp, with battery powered high-intensity l.e.d.s. That, coupled with a bright bicycle rear-light stitched to the reflective Sam Browne belt I planned to wear would, with luck, get me by. I know that such would not comply strictly with current Construction and Use requirements, but they appeared to be excellent bits of tackle and surely better than the option of the period acetylene gas lamps originally fitted to H. However, I needed to be sure that the headlight would survive the low-frequency vibrations of an early single-cylinder Triumph. To test this I fitted it to *H* and rode around Yorkshire a bit. It passed with flying colours. On reflection, it was unfortunate that had I removed it before I took the bike to the Graham Walker Run at Beaulieu in Hampshire a week or two before I departed for France and forgot to re-fit it. Rats, I thought, I will have to buy another. Leaving *H* on the car park, I drove the kilometre or so into Les Gets centre, where I thought I had seen a bike shop. I was correct in this, but they specialised in mountain bikes for downhill racing and did not stock lighting at all, nor could they suggest anywhere else nearby. 'Morzine, perhaps' was the best they could offer. This area is the global centre of the sport of destroying expensive high-tech bikes by rushing implausibly fast down mountainsides. It also helps the local orthopaedic surgeons to keep their hands in during the lulls between ski seasons. I guess it is just as well that the cycle sport is conducted entirely in daylight. I drew a few more Euros from a nearby cash machine and resolved to buy a headlight if I passed a branch of the equivalent of Halfords on my way south.

All was not lost! In the van I keep a torch, for emergencies. This is a circular sort of l.e.d. inspection lamp which I had got as a free gift from B & Q. It has a folding plastic hook on the back of it. I could see no way of fitting it securely to the bike, but slipped it into my pocket anyway. That, plus a small reflector on the rear mudguard, was my lighting kit. My other main act of compliance was a motorcycle-size 'GB' plate which I had made when I started to participate in foreign rallies. It is white on black and doesn't look out of keeping with the rest of the bike. Oh, yes ... and while I am in France I try and ride down the right-hand side of the road, which I find avoids endless unpleasantness.

It is mandatory to carry the registration document for the vehicle with you at all times when motoring in France, so naturally I had *H*'s papers. It had been impressed upon me that the penalty for not doing so is a substantial on-the-spot fine and seizure of the vehicle. It was a shame that I had slipped them into the Ipad's case for safe keeping. Fortunately for my peace of mind I didn't think of this until almost the end of my ride.

Once I reckoned I had checked as much as possible I realised that I had run out of excuses and it was time to ride away for as long as it would take to get to the Med and back. I confess it took a certain effort of will to do that, but once I joined the Route des Grandes Alpes at the little roundabout in front of which I had drunk beer the previous evening, my fears left me and I settled into the ride. This was typical. Each morning I would feel a bit apprehensive about setting off, but as soon as *H* had warmed up and I had settled into the saddle I would become completely at ease and relaxed as the even thump of the motor bowled us along the next stage of our small adventure.

I may go out tomorrow if I can borrow a coat to wear ... I slotted *H* into top gear for the run down the gorge. It was a beautiful day. Next stop Cluses.

The road here is fairly main-ish, but the traffic was not heavy and I was familiar with it from previous holidays. There are some great views as the road descends through hairpins into the village of Taninges. If you fancy an interesting diversion this early on, you can turn left there and make a big loop via Samöens, but I was keen to get to some *real* passes, so I pressed on to Cluses, where I stopped at a likely looking tyre supplier to beg a blast of the airline to bring *H*'s rear tyre up to pressure. The fitter could not have been more helpful and we went off confidently, knowing that there was 2.8 Bar in both ends.

Suddenly it dawned on me that I was on roads that I had never travelled before and it was up to nobody but me to keep going. Curiously I found this pretty liberating and revelled on the long climb up and over the Col de la Colombière to Le Grand-Bornand, a ski resort town that is not notably grand, I thought, although I am sure it must perk up considerably when there is plenty of snow about. The Col de la Colombière gives a fair foretaste of what is to come. It is the first climb to more than 1500 metres and the first to rise above the tree-line and reach the rocks and high pastures. Then the Col des Aravis (1486m / 4875ft) involved a bit more hard work for *H*, but she was coping wonderfully and I don't think that bottom gear was ever called for: second served well for everything we were meeting. Once over the Aravis I felt the mood of the Route somehow changed. We were into country which began to feel remote; subtly different to the France I was familiar with.

The next point of passage I had noted on my minimal route instruction was 'N.-D de Bellcombe', the name that appears on the Michelin map. I am ashamed to admit that I did not know what the 'N.-D' signified. I even felt a frisson of anticipation about finding out – how sad is that? After more pretty vigorous climbing the village signboard came into view and all was revealed: *Notre Dame de Bellecombe*. To drive the message home there was a statue of what I assumed was the Madonna in a lay-by. I mentally kicked myself for having missed the obvious and stopped to take a photo. The statue turned out to be of an old chap in a robe striking a pose.

Not *the Madonna*

The roads here are narrow – particularly in the villages – and for obvious reasons road maintenance is done during the warmer months, so one-way working with temporary traffic lights was frequent. At first I was reluctant to let the motor stop because I was uncertain how *H*'s carburettor would respond to the altitude when needing to restart in a hurry. I need not have bothered because she was happy to be brought back to life with one swing of the kickstart lever every time. We are perpetually surrounded by mountain scenery here and it is surprising how quickly one gets accustomed to it. However, as soon as one is south of the little town of Bellcombe it becomes even more spectacular, with the panorama of the Gorge d'Arly. Well worth a stop. Then it was on to the Col des Saisies (1650m/5413ft) which was deserted apart from a parked white van attended by a very pleasant young English woman who told me she was driving the support vehicle for a group of cyclists riding the Grandes Alpes. She admired *H* and I was offered refreshment in the form of a Kit-Kat bar to go with my bottle of water. It made a nice interlude before riding on down through many lacets to Belfort, where we fuelled-up. Now for the assault on the Cormet de Roselende. This is a serious pass. Why is it a *Cormet* and not a *Col*? What distinguishes a cormet from a col? Just what is a cormet anyway? Apparently there is no difference. Neither of my French/English dictionaries offers any help and an exhaustive trawl of the internet simply had me repeatedly being asked whether I meant 'cornet' or 'coronet'. Anyway, it was a beautiful 20 kilometre second-gear climb up past a vast lake to the shoulder (1963m /6440ft).

Just before the summit I stopped at a veranda bar to give *H* a rest and me a drink. A group of cycle riders were taking a well-deserved breather here too, and we soon got talking. We mutually admired the vastness and majesty of the view. I am full of admiration for those who pedal their way over the Alps. I don't think I could have managed it at any time of my life. The group were all English as far as I could tell and asked where I was from. 'Yorkshire'.

A couple of them volunteered that they were also based there and we chatted on. One was a retired fireman, recently moved to Settle from Leeds. Little bells rang faraway in the misty depths my brain; 'Did you use to fly paragliders?' 'Yes!' – It was an old acquaintance from the Dales Hang Gliding and Paragliding club, Robin Moore. This was all a pleasure, but I guess it should not have been too much of a surprise because once you have got a love of mountains, any excuse will do to spend some time among them.

And yes, it was Mandy whom I had encountered with their support vehicle back at Les Saisies. She is English, but based in Chamonix and works for the tour organiser. Naturally she knows the Alps from top to bottom and sideways too.

Early on during my run I wore the reflective Sam Browne belt, which I can't argue was the sensible thing to do. However, I soon got irritated with the way it would slip into off-the-shoulder mode and resorted to lashing it to the back of the bike as conspicuously as possible.

I paused again a kilometre or so further on, to take a photo at the marker board at the top of the Col. A lot of people were there and I became engaged in conversation with two Swiss couples touring together, driving immaculate Peugeot convertibles with

Pinin Farina bodywork. From the 1970s or '80s, I guess. We were all getting a similar degree of delight in our aged vehicles in spite of their fundamental differences and *H*'s less-than-immaculate turn-out. There was a stall at the top, selling Savoyard delicacies, including the celebrated Beaufort cheese. The proprietor came out to have a chat and admire the vehicles. He is the man in the photo.

Beaufort cheese, monsieur?

At the start of the day I had thought that I would do well to reach Bourg-St-Maurice, at the southern foot of the Roselende, but that turned out to be easy. I was feeling really good and decided to press on to Val d'Isère. The road is straightforward all the way, even though it is a good climb up to Tignes, where I nearly took the wrong road, across the top of the giant dam, the Barrage de Tignes. Eventually, in the early evening, *H* and I chugged up the main street of Val d'Isère and caught the tourist office just before it closed. I was rather relieved by that because the town seems pretty isolated and very few hotels or businesses were functioning. The lady in the office pointed us in the right direction and a few minutes later *H* was being tucked away outside the Hotel Bellville and I looked forward to dinner. I was rather nervous about having to leave her outside and fitted the bicycle cable-lock which, with a certain foresight, I had remembered to bring with me. My confidence would have been greater if I had remembered to bring the key with me too. However, I defy anyone to spot that the cable is not actually locked fully around anything once it has artfully been placed into position with its tangle of coils, so it has at least a certain deterrent and delaying function, locked-up or not.

Val d'Isère is very much a ski centre and one feels that not a lot happens there in September. I chatted to an elderly gent who seemed delighted by *H*'s appearance in his town. He turned out to be the local priest and we both dined in the Bellville's restaurant most satisfactorily. I got the impression that there was little alternative!

Day's distance approx 120miles/200km

Chapter 6
Starting to get serious

Val d'Isere to La Salle-les-Alpes via three major climbs

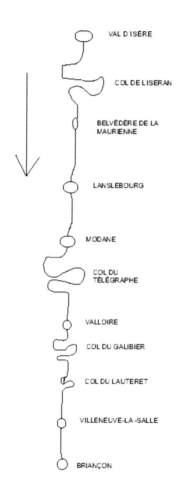

I remembered seeing a filling station on my way into Val d'Isere and rode back there to fuel-up before tackling what I thought of as the first really serious day of my trip: the Col de L'Iseran. The highest of the passes on the Touring Club's original *Route*. Sure enough, the nature of the terrain changed as soon as I left the town and we rode into pure mountain scenery. The ascent was shaded this morning and I debated whether to put my big coat on, but decided against it as the sky was blue above the mountain tops. Naturally, I slipped into a chorus or two of Simon Smith and the amazing dancing bear; particularly the bit about *if I can borrow a coat to wear*, but soon forgot about it as the climb developed and I concentrated on coaxing *H* forever upwards. Tunes played a much smaller part in this journey than they had on my earlier adventure when we did John o' Groats to Land's End and back again. I think there were two main reasons for this: the roads in the Alps require more concentration for more of the time and also I was now wearing an open-face pudding-basin type crash helmet. This is far less conducive to my form of tuneless song than its fully enclosed counterpart.

The Iseran is a climb among rocks. *H* coped wonderfully and we rose up through the lunar landscape non-stop and with no real difficulty for the best part of an hour. My confidence grew with every bend and shortly after a particularly tight right-hander we climbed the final metres and burst into the sunlight on an open parking area. It was flanked by one or two severe stone-built buildings and the iconic signboard claiming that we were at 2770metres (9,087ft). I had felt a bit chilly during the latter part of the climb and was reminded that this was seriously high by the ice on a few shaded puddles.

On the way up I had been passed by quite a few motorcycles, hardly surprising in view of *H*'s necessarily stately progress – the only things we overtake are hikers and the less-athletic pedal cyclists – but I was surprised by just what a large congregation of bikers was present at the top. A group of Italians waved and shouted and came up to me as soon as I had stopped. While I was pulling *H* onto the stand one of them was telling me about a similar Triumph he owned, but that he didn't realise that it would be able to cope with the Route des Grandes Alpes. This turned out to be Sirio Lanfranchini, a great enthusiast and fluent English speaker whom I plan to meet again on other motorcycle adventures. He owns the successor to the Model H, which has essentially the same engine and frame but uses chain rather than belt for the final drive. It is the Model SD, the *SD* standing for 'Spring Drive'. It was introduced in 1922 and the name was to reassure the conservative motorcycle purchasers of the day that the transmission harshness which blighted of some of Triumph's early chain-driven competitors had been overcome. Altogether a magic interlude, giving me a sense of delight which would remain with me for the next couple of weeks.

Making friends at the summit

The descent from the Col de L'Iseran took us into the valley of the river Arc, with glorious panoramas all the way, particularly around the Belvédère de la Maurienne and on through Bonneval-sur-Arc. I let *H* descend fairly gingerly, as usual, chugging down in second gear most of the way and pulling the exhaust-valve lifter to shed a little more speed at hairpin bends. This is quite a contrast to the average motorcyclist on the road, equipped with all those things which *H* lacks, such as roadholding and brakes and an iPod piping stereo into a full-face helmet. It may sound like a hardship, but for me it is not a problem. Oh, yes, of course on a swift machine I can still enjoy blasting down a strip of tarmac punctuated by the exhilaration of scraping from verge-to-verge as quickly as possible at the bends, but on *H* I chug along drinking all the scenery in, occasionally dreaming dreams and relishing every second. In fact, the time often passes too quickly.

Before long we were in the little town of Lanslebourg where we stopped for a snack lunch. Looking around the shop I got really lucky and found just the book I needed: Michelin's *Les Alpes à Moto*. It contains narratives of all the major touring routes as well as a very good detachable map with them all clearly marked. There are also pages of Tulip-rally type route instructions and info for GPS users. Personally I much prefer to stick to using the map as you get to hold a much better picture of the route in your mind, but that is just personal taste. I had been a bit surprised how little literature I could find on the subject, but this book did the job almost perfectly. For my immediate purposes there were a couple of minor snags in that it is written as if you have started on the Med and are going north, and it uses, not unreasonably, French throughout. I will use this as the excuse for all my subsequent navigation errors. The mountain on the left entering Lanslebourg is Mont Cenis and in the middle of the town you may turn across a little bridge and attack the Col du Mt Cenis, up which in a few kilometres you will find yourself very high and in Italy. As this is not strictly on the itinerary of the Route, which remains within France, I did not make the diversion, choosing instead to carry on down the valley of the river Arc to Modane. This is a busy east-west trade route through the Alps. The Route follows the main road, but I managed to find the very minor D83 which is vaguely parallel and delivers you to Modane via a road *touristique et panoramique*. Recommended. Modane itself was larger and more full of railway lines and freight operations than I had expected. Riding through the town I was overtaken by a small group of classic bikes on German plates being ridden in a spirited manner. They looked as if they were from the 1950s. A further 20 kilometres of main-ish going took me to St-Michel-de-Maurienne and a left turn to the Cols du Télégraphe and Galibier, two formidable climbs which have a particular resonance for any follower of the Tour de France. On the way I was overtaken again by the same group of classics, still being ridden in a lively but slightly disorganised manner.

At 1565m (5134ft) the Col du Télégraphe is not particularly high, but still presents a fair challenge after the mild gradients of the valley. I enjoyed the steady ride up through forested hillsides punctuated with small sunny clearings. As we climbed *H* took me effortlessly past dozens of cyclists.

The original télégraphe was a Napoleonic mechanical semaphore device installed on the fort at the top in 1801 as an early-warning aid along the Franco-Italian border. It was apparently both practical and useful, surviving until the 1850s, when it was overtaken by the electric telegraph.

Now for the Col du Galibier, which would be a new experience for me. We fuelled up with four litres at Valloire and pressed on. At 2701m (8861ft) the Galibier has a serious reputation and is usually one of the last passes to open in spring and the first to close in autumn. It is often the highest point reached during the Tour de France. We were soon above the tree-line and the views and sense of exposure are as fine as you will find anywhere. The road is a masterpiece, but be aware that if vertigo is a problem for you the Galibier may not be entirely to your taste. Near the top there is a tunnel, but for the full experience you should avoid this and stay on the open road all the way. *H* managed well, but we did need bottom gear for a short distance near the top.

These old side-valve machines get extremely hot under such going and apart from making sure that the oil supply is maintained, there is not much else you can do to help, apart from stopping for occasional rests. The right-hand side of the motor is the worst-affected and that is exactly where the footrest puts my right calf. Consequently on the stiffer passes I must have looked pretty untidy with my leg being waved around in the meagre slipstream while we attacked corner after corner.

We eventually arrived at the top to a round of applause, much of it from other bikers who had passed us at the bottom and obviously didn't give much for our chances. Among these was the group of classic riders which had whistled past me leaving Modane. Naturally we were soon discussing bikes together. Their machines were superbly turned out. I was impressed by a 250cc Simson, which is virtually a copy of the R27 BMW of the period: it looked as if it had just left the factory. However, I was told that it had disgraced itself the day before when a main bearing had failed in a big way. They had managed to strip it out and replace it with a bearing obtained locally, all within the day. I was well impressed.

The group was from an 'oldtimer' club in the region of the old German Democratic Republic and all their bikes were originally from Eastern Europe. They were working to a tight time schedule and revealingly one of them remarked that he envied me being alone because they were too many to make good progress – always somebody getting lost or breaking down!

From the Galibier the Route continues south towards Briançon, described in some guides as the highest city in Europe. I guess it rather depends on exactly what constitutes a 'city' and I think it barely scrapes in. In the old days the requirement was to have a cathedral, but in the new European Community it appears that a supermarket will suffice. Just when I had got nicely into the rhythm of the Galibier descent it came as a surprise to meet traffic lights on the side of a mountain. These give priority to vehicles which have used the tunnel and I had to summon up all of *H*'s meagre braking capability to stop in time. After that call to attention the rest of the ride was easy. However, there was another pass to negotiate on the way: the Col du Lautaret. This has none of the character of the previous passes and the descent from the Galibier delivers you almost at the top of it. By the standards I was becoming used to, this scarcely counts as a pass, being part of the main road from Grenoble to Briançon, but there are good views and soon the town appears in the distance down the valley, a jumble of ramparts and fortifications. I planned to stop overnight at one of the villages which now serve the winter-sports region of Serre Chavalier, before getting tangled up in the town itself. This plan worked out well. It had been a hard day in the saddle and I was ready to rest.

Approx 100miles/160km

Chapter 7

I wonder where I shall end up tonight?

When I set out each morning I have a vague idea of where I hope to get to during the day's riding, but never book in advance. This demands frequent acts of faith and generally it works out quite well. My basic rules are to start looking early and not to rely too much on first impressions. My budget does not extend to five-star establishments and I wouldn't care to stay in them if it did. Provided I can get a room with a comfortable bed, en-suite facilities are a bonus. It helps that I usually make my trips during school term-times to avoid peak holiday seasons. The Alps is a well-developed tourist area and on my journey through I had no trouble getting into small hotels, all of them with greater or lesser degree of character. Earlier in the year when I was riding through mainly rural areas of northern France and Belgium, I found it much more difficult.

This day, I had Briançon as my target. I thought it was a bit optimistic perhaps, but with the Galibier in the bag and then the Lauteret, I knew I could do it. I already had a working knowledge of Briançon because Rob, one of my adventurous sons, had lived there for a couple of years before he moved away from Europe and I had visited him there. I knew that I would be better off staying out of the town itself, so started keeping an eye open along the Guisane valley which leads into Briançon beneath the mountain ridge of Serre Chavalier, a well-known ski area. The scattering of villages along it now caters mainly for that trade and are quiet in the sunnier months. I found the tourist office in one of them, Villeneuve la Salle, where a charming young woman handed me a

50

brochure with a selection of hotels to choose from. I picked *Le Chatelas*, simply because it was 'biker-friendly' and very nearby. It turned out to be an excellent choice, although the initial signs were not particularly encouraging.

Le Chatelas has character. I could sympathise with anyone who may be daunted by the excess of character, but believe me, it is worth sticking with it. I was shown to room 5 which had a large comfy bed and a view across the Guisane river to a decaying sheet iron shed onto which a large tree had collapsed. The un-squashed part of the shed was still being used. Let me make it clear that the shed and hotel were unrelated. The room's en-suite facilities were provided in the form of a lavatory which proclaimed itself in capital letters suitable for reading at fifteen paces to be WATERFLUSH ACTANA 700. It was set at a jaunty angle beside a satisfactory hand-basin. If things had been left at that there would have been space to spare, but at some time an upgrade had been attempted which involved manoeuvring a spacious shower cubicle into slightly less room than was available. At the planning stage a moment's work with a tape-rule would have revealed that the existing concertina door would no longer close properly, and, more disturbingly, if one managed to shut it using just the right blend of brute force and artifice, it would vigorously resist any attempt from inside to get it open again. Kept me entertained for some time after I had showered-off the day's travel. I never again attempted to close it. After that, it was with some trepidation that I presented myself for dinner at the appointed hour.

Ordering dinner at Le Chatelas is a simple matter of being guided to a table and sitting down. The tiresome business of wrestling with a French menu and making a considered selection is completely bypassed. You sit down and dinner comes. Heaven help you if you are a vegetarian. Today it was pasta soup, then a slab of braised steak more tender and delicious than I could have imagined, served with fresh vegetables and potatoes which tasted just like the home-grown ones I remember as a nipper 70 years ago. Dessert was chocolate mousse and then dream cheese to end up with. I couldn't imagine a better way of refuelling after a fairly long day in the saddle. Naturally, I allowed digestion to be encouraged by some local red wine.

The decor of the dining room is interesting. It can best be described as a collection, or perhaps an *accumulation*. It is just full of the strange, the interesting, the artistic, the kitsch and the simply old, in no particular order. There was no shortage of conversation pieces and soon I was in conversation with Helge, a biker from Germany, whose immaculate BMW KR750 was parked outside.

Note to English readers: that is Helg*e*, a male name and not to be confused with Helg*a* the time-expired chorus girl from the opening scene of *Cabaret* whose muscular thighs and picturesquely torn net stockings have haunted me for a generation.

Helge had served for many years in the American Zone of Berlin and spoke excellent English. He was a good companion and soon we were swapping stories of motorcycle trips over much of Europe. Eventually, with the inevitability of such matters, we lit upon the subject of regional drinks and so I was introduced to Genepi – the liqueur of the Savoy Alps. It is rather like a less-treacley version of Chartreuse and most palatable after a good meal. I managed to choke down a couple with little difficulty, purely in the interests of research, you understand.

Back in my room admiring the Waterflush Actana 700 again, I received a phone call from my other adventurous son, Matthew. He is based near Stuttgart and was keeping me updated with the European weather situation. The bad news was that a front would pass through the Alps any minute, bringing rain and low cloud. I could cope with rain but didn't fancy our next big ascent, the Col d'Isoard, in cloud. The good news was that the front would be through in 24 hours and the weather behind it was set fair. I prepared myself for a second night at Le Chatelas if the sky was as grim as predicted in the morning.

Waking, I noted that the mountains towering above the tin shed were cloaked in fog and decided to make the best of a day of enforced leisure. After breakfast, I strolled out into the local approximation of a main street to take stock of the broader weather situation before deciding on my game plan for the day. I noted that although there was no shortage of cloud well below mountain-top level, rain didn't really seem to be in the offing, although fortunately I was sceptical enough to roll up my waterproof coat and pack it into an old helmet bag I had with me. I would, I decided, stroll to the post office at the other end of the village for stamps, then continue on along the valley on a rustic footpath to the centre of Briançon for a little gentle shopping. It didn't start well because I was served with a marked lack of grace at the post office due to my having nothing smaller than a twenty Euro note. As I strolled on, it gradually emerged that there were some basic flaws in my basic plan. I won't go into the finest details, but put simply it was at least twice as far to town as I had imagined and my weather forecasting lacked precision. Also, the rustic footpath ended on the outskirts of the town and the final kilometres are shared intimately with lots of traffic.

Briançon has never struck me as a town of great beauty, or indeed any at all. It is dominated by a citadel reached via the Avenue de la République, which is dead straight and dauntingly steep if on foot. After my morning's trudge punctuated by the occasional shower, I didn't fancy a further challenge and chose to stay down in the lower, commercial, part of town. I was pleased to find a bookshop which had a small English-language section. The choice was decidedly limited and I settled on *One Shot*, by Lee Child. I confess that I had assumed the author was a woman until quite recently and had mentally filed his books, unread, along with Danielle Steele and Catherine Cookson. The hero is Jack Reacher, a taciturn six-foot-five ex-military man who strides the States anonymously while thinning out the baddies. I enjoyed it, but while writing this book the film of One Shot was released with Tom Cruise as the lead. I have not yet seen it, but they must use some pretty creative camera angles to make Cruise look much above five-foot-six, let alone six-five!

Even if rain had not set in, I would not have wished to repeat the morning's walk. The bus back to the Hotel Chatelas departed from the train station yard. The service was infrequent and I found myself with an hour or so to pass – not a great hardship with reasonable chairs, a coffee machine to hand and a book to read. After a short while I realised that my presence was not being ignored. Apparently my perfectly practical outfit of breeches and waistcoat, topped with a well-run-in Australian drover's coat was a source of wonder to an elderly couple on the other side of the booking hall. OK, maybe it is a bit odd. Eventually it was too much for the wife, a solid person cast in the mould of a second-row forward, who despatched her husband on a mission to inspect and report. He duly came and stood about a metre away while checking me over from head to foot in an extraordinarily unselfconscious manner. I felt like an exhibit. I did briefly wonder if he was an agent from the Style & Fashion Police but the evidence was against it. He could kindly be described as portly and was wearing a baseball cap suggesting he supported the New York Yankees, something I thought improbable. He stayed long enough for me to get my notebook out and catalogue the rest of his outfit: bright green anorak, khaki cargo shorts stopping two inches below the knee, beige socks to three inches above the ankle and black all-terrain sandals. He did not respond to a nervous smile and made no attempt at communication, managing throughout to give an impression of severe disapproval. I still don't know what his conclusions were, but he was obviously deficient in the irony department.

I was amazed at the distance of the bus ride back. Had I really walked so far?

After another grand feed, chicken this time, among the bric-a-brac, I settled in bed and in the peaceful moments between putting down my diary and falling asleep, I contemplated the Waterflush Actana 700 and wondered why the designer had felt the need to label it quite so boldly. I can respect pride in achievement in the world of domestic ceramics, but I believe labelling should serve a purpose. In this example it eluded me. Maybe the marketing department thought that after a particularly comforting bowel movement the user would subliminally give thanks to the Actana 700 and immediately think 'We must have one of these at home', but I am not entirely convinced. I slept dreamlessly.

When I woke next morning, the sky was mainly blue above the mountains. Admittedly there were also some clouds which I thought were moving in a pretty spirited manner, but I put them to the back of my mind and knew I would be on the road again.

Mileage on bike: 0

Mileage on foot: Lots

Chapter 8
Keeping at it

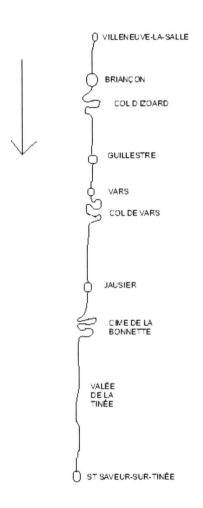

VILLENEUVE-LA-SALLE

BRIANÇON

COL D IZOARD

GUILLESTRE

VARS

COL DE VARS

JAUSIER

CIME DE LA
BONNETTE

VALÉE
DE LA
TINÉE

ST SAVEUR-SUR-TINÉE

There is no subtlety about the approach to the Col de l'Izoard. Just follow a couple of signposts in Briançon and the ascent starts almost as soon as the houses stop. Going across the town, the wind caught me at road junctions – on a Model H, like most bikes of the period which combine light weight and upright posture, you can expect to be moved around a bit in gusts. There is a certain satisfaction in learning to anticipate them and maintain a straight course almost regardless of what is being chucked at you. At least it was dry, but it was cool enough for me to be glad I had my big coat on. I was also comforted by the knowledge that one of its pockets held a small bottle of whisky which I had been given back at the hotel just before I set off. It was a gift from a couple of Scottish riders on modern bikes with whom I had been chatting while getting ready. I now regret that I was so preoccupied that I forgot to ask their names, which was rather unforgivable of me. So, now, if by any chance you should read this, a hearty public 'thank-you' gentlemen!

My Scottish benefactors

The Col is a tough climb by any standards. *H* and I flogged steadily uphill, first through trees and then into a very exposed mountain landscape. I loved it until I sensed the start of the dreaded belt-slip on exiting from a tight corner. Soddit. I coaxed *H* on until we found a sheltered spot where we stopped and I hauled her onto the stand. There was a simple explanation for the slip: neglect on my behalf. *H* had been running so well that I had overlooked a bit of simple maintenance which I normally perform every hundred miles or so. I had neglected to wipe the belt. This is necessary because the art of the oil-seal was still at the primitive stage in 1918 and there is a slight but persistent escape of gearbox lubricant which finds its way onto the driving pulley and thence onto the belt. A good wipe with a petrol-soaked rag sorts it out and I had to perform that ritual by the roadside. We were soon on the way again.

You know when you are getting near the summit of these big climbs because the names of the Tour de France stars appear whitewashed onto the road surface with increasing frequency. By September they are fading a bit, as sadly, is the reputation of some of the stars as more and more drug confessions emerge. Personally, I find it hard to imagine how anyone manages to cycle up these mountains at all, doped or not. I would need vast quantities of illicit chemical assistance to pedal up one col on a bike, let alone *race* over three in a single day.

The top of Col de l'Izoard has, in my opinion, an element of savagery in the landscape which was missing from the earlier climbs. Not even the Iseran or Galibier quite match it for exposure and sheer desolation! Again I was reminded of the way the temperature drops with altitude. Very roughly you should expect it to drop one degree Celsius for each hundred metres climbed. It had been cool when I left Briançon that morning – I guess about 10° at the most. As the Col involves an ascent of more than a thousand metres, the ice on the puddles outside the large refuge at the top was not unexpected. I was aware of one more oversight in my preparation, in that I had left my nice warm gloves at home and had only a pair of unlined soft leather ones of a type favoured by fighter pilots. When new they had been white-ish and after several years have taken on a colour and character of their own which defies description. I like them very much, but they leave a lot to be desired in sub-zero conditions.

Down in the warmer gorge of the Combe de Queras I found myself following a large Romanian artic which was travelling within inches of rock faces and through small tunnels in which I would have sworn it was an interference fit. It sailed through with inches to spare – certainly less than a foot. I was spellbound at the driver's skill and judgement and wondered how many times he had driven this route to gain such confidence. My opinion changed rapidly when eventually, amid a small shower of shattered trailer roof, he managed to jam it securely at a tight left-hander with a rocky overhang. First time, I imagine.

I knew *H* was getting ready for fuel and made a detour to get a fill-up at the Intermarché on the main road near Guillestre. It turned out to be a good call as we took on 5.3 litres, which meant we were down to vapour and rust particles. Guillestre is just off the Route, but it is a lovely little town and well worth the effort of a visit for a coffee and a pastry before continuing on D902 over the Col de Vars (2109m/6920ft).

Vars was a steady climb, but not difficult and we made it to the top without a stop. The evening before I had read that Hannibal had come this way with his army and war elephants on his mission to set about the Romans, although historians argue over this and many think that he turned left at Briançon and aimed toward Turin. However I was better persuaded that Francis the First of France really did take his army through Vars in 1515, prior to having it out with the Swiss near Milan at the battle of Marignano. *Never 'eard of 'im*, I thought, having had a typical English education which was restricted to British monarchs and battles in which we led the winning side, such as Agincourt a hundred years earlier when Sir Laurence Olivier thrashed the Frogs. Francis' route is better documented than Hannibal's and his army was impressive by any standards: at least 40 heavy cannon, 25,000 cavalry and 70,000 infantrymen. As I kept the commotion of *H*'s single cylinder organised and we climbed steadily, I wondered at the logistics of moving such a force over the underdeveloped Alpine tracks of the middle-ages. I bet the citizens of Vars looked upon its passage as a very mixed blessing. Nowadays this is the heart of a winter-sports playground, but they are prepared for that annual sporting invasion.

Descent of Col du Vars

The Col de Vars was really only punctuation on our way to the next big one: the Col de la Bonette! I went through Jausiers, a small town where you make the decision to go right or left. Left is south-east, while right is south-west. Either way counts as belonging to the Route des Grandes Alpes, but I decided to go left for the Col de la Bonette rather than right, via the Col de la Cayolle. Regardless of choice, you end up in the Valley of the Tigne and all points to Menton. I wanted to go over the Bonette, the highest paved road in all the Alps and had become rather focused on it. So focused, in fact, that I can recall nothing at all of Jausiers. I count that as a bit of a failure really, because I like to take in as much as I can and not become too involved in hitting targets.

The Bonette was a long ascent. On the way to the 2802m (9250ft) pass *H* struggled a bit and I resorted to the old trick of weaving up the road to reduce the effective gradient. This technique is a fairly desperate measure and strictly for use only when there is no other traffic at all. We climbed well and I was able to stay in second gear until the final kilometre or two, when a shift to bottom was essential. Bearing in mind that officially 'high altitude' is considered to start at 2400m and that humans start to be affected by lack of oxygen from as low as 1500m, I think *H* does very well. When I planned this journey (I use 'planned' in the very loosest sense of the word) I was concerned that there would be insufficient power at altitude and that I would have to juggle constantly with the fuel mixture in the carburettor. I need not have worried. *H*'s very simple carb coped superbly and during almost all of our time in the Alps, all I had to do was to set the air lever wide open so she could gulp in as much oxygen as possible. I devised a sophisticated automatic 'full-air' device en route to ensure this. It consisted of an elastic band cut from an old inner-tube looped around the air lever and hooked on to the horn clamp. Only occasionally, when I sensed the old dear may have been tending to overheat under pressure, would I override the rubber band to richen the mixture briefly. Worked a treat.

Close to the summit the road follows a long traverse amid open bare terrain. *H* was feeling the height a bit and wouldn't sustain the pull in second gear when the incline steepened, and I had to reach for bottom. At times like that you most earnestly hope that the belt won't slip. Of course, it slipped. Not even vigorous footing on my behalf helped and I knew that I could not postpone the inevitable, and anyway, at above 8,000ft my leg effort was unlikely to be sustained for any length of time either. I heaved the bike onto the stand and whipped a link out of the belt as well as giving it a swift wipe with a petrol-soaked rag. It probably took no more than five minutes, but on this draughty mountainside it did seem like a bit of a chore.

Perhaps I should take a moment here to explain that keeping the belt gripping in marginal circumstances calls for a skill similar to that of coaxing a car up a snowy incline. It is important to hang on to as high a gear as possible consistent with maintaining upward progress: you just know that a change down will probably break traction and leave you stuck.

Once proceeding under power again, I narrowly avoided turning left into a small tunnel enigmatically marked *Turin* which would have cut out the final hairpin, and very shortly found myself at the summit monument. I felt vaguely heroic for having beaten this 2,800+ metre col, but was soon brought down to earth by the presence of a large tourist coach with its inevitable complement of camera-snapping tourists, and several cyclists who were not even breathing heavily. It was distinctly fresh at the top and the Michelin book's comments on the permanent glacial wind were completely justified.

The day was completely blue and the views astonishing. Waves of mountain everywhere. Great ranges of France and Italy spreading away to the limits of vision. There is a monument at the top of the La Bonette pass, built when it was opened in 1961. Once a mule-track, then improved under Napoleon, it is now claimed to be the highest through-road for wheeled traffic in France and is undoubtedly a magnificent example of highway engineering, but I can't help thinking that the route was chosen to a certain extent by a desire to get above that magic 2,800 metre mark – a feat which it apparently manages by just the height of a rather tall man!

Col de la Bonette: It really is a big coat,

Nothing brings you back down to earth faster than meeting a tourist coach at the top of what you imagined was a heroic conquest!

The route down called for no more than the patience required to lower a marginally brakeless motorcycle down an extraordinarily big hill with a succession of unguarded bends. It sounds as if it should be tedious, but I love it. There I am, in the heart of the Alps with sections of the road visible for miles ahead, curving and twisting downwards. Some of the surface stands out, accented by the sun; other sections disappear around shoulders of the hillside or into black tunnels. Instead of being just a spectator or mundane user of the road, I become related to the landscape in a way which is peculiar to the rider of an old slow motorcycle.

I cannot blast down the straights and anchor up with squealing tyres for the corners. I cannot revel in the exhaust howl of a four-cylinder fuel-injected crotch-rocket echoing off sheer rock. What I can do is sit relaxed and simply absorb the magic of the mountains, with an occasional nod of thanks to the brilliance of the road engineers who made it all possible. Oh, yes, and some thanks also to the memory of the craftsmen at the old Triumph factory in Coventry who, at the height of a war almost a century ago, constructed *H*, my time machine.

We passed through a creepy abandoned village which I assume was part of a military station at one time, were cheered by a couple of men roofing a chalet a kilometre or so further on and eventually joined the course of the river Tinée. I was glad to find a room at a pleasant hotel at St Saveur du Tinée. It had been a long day and rather cool towards the end. My room was up three floors and heaven knows how many stairs, but I was soon comfortably installed and made my way down to the dining room for dinner.

Trace the road; just a fraction of the descent from LaBonette

The dining room eventually became a sort of casual social centre as travellers of the Route from many countries compared notes. Frank and Christina from Heidelberg were entertained by the contrast between *H* and their BMW 1600GT. Next morning I was to share a table with a Canadian couple who had just dropped in for breakfast. They were doing it all on foot, carrying basic camping gear!

Approx 108miles/172km

Chapter 9
To the Med

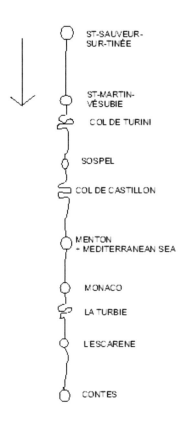

Friday September 14

Frank and Christina from Heidelberg.
H was a total contrast to their 1600cc, 6-cylinder BMW!

We left St Saveur after a modest photo session in the backyard of the pub. I find loading up is always a vaguely exhausting business and am paranoid about leaving something behind. Anyway, there were no problems today; *H* fired up easily and we motored away towards the south. The fun started early on with conquest of the Col de St Martin. At 1500m (4920ft) this is not particularly spectacular as it is wooded virtually all the way, but it made for a good start to what was to be a pretty vigorous day in the saddle. As soon as the descent began I could feel a change in the climate which could not be attributed to sunlight alone.

Maybe it was my imagination, but I believe I was sensing the start of the Mediterranean influence. It didn't yet smell like maritime air, but neither was it completely Alpine.

A lot of road repairing goes on during summer in the Alps and quite long stretches of one-way alternate working are common. I thought this idea of incorporating a count-down timer on the temporary lights was brilliant. Here I know there is a 25-second wait before the green.

I was looking forward to motoring over an old friend: the Col de Turini, (1607m, 5272ft). This col has long featured in the Monte Carlo Rally, usually as one of the special tests after the cars have first reached Monte. At the end of the 1950s I had been a member of a service crew from the Mintex brake lining company and had motored over it in a Standard Vanguard. I recall little apart from lots of bends and lots of snow, but then it was the depths of winter. Tackled in the dark by exhausted crews, the Turini had a reputation for sorting out the field and I wanted to see what it really looked like from the saddle of a slow ancient motorcycle.

The Turini was indeed hard work and my diary records *very tough*. But it was also great and very satisfying in spite of not being spectacularly high. I stopped for refreshment in the tiny village at the top – *Orangina* and a sandwich – and felt pretty pleased with myself. On my long runs I usually avoid alcohol at lunchtime, which may surprise some of my old chums, but it is important to keep as sharp as possible when riding *H*. Although she covers the ground quite slowly, she demands attention every metre of the way. This is not a bike upon which you can ride hands-off for more than a second or so because the slightest irregularity in road surface will have those long handlebars swinging all over the place.

I had made a note to make a small detour near the top of the Turini, to the *Refuge of the Camp d'Argent*, from which the first views of the sea appear. Apparently these views are well worth the slight effort. I write *apparently* because I now had the bit firmly between my teeth and the thought of actually reaching the coast was acting as a powerful magnet. I mention the Camp d'Argent simply in the hope that other bikers will be inspired to make the effort.

Descending the Col de Turini, the temperature rose steadily and I thought it would be little more than a formality to reach the sea. We motored easily through Sospel and then met the Col de Castillon. Although only 707m (2320ft) it is a steep little bugger and my notebook records *surprisingly tough*! If I had looked at my map a little more closely I would have noticed that those chevrons which indicate steep gradient feature fairly prominently on both sides of it. Bottom gear was called for.

Soon the sea was appearing frequently between the hills and the trees and I found myself joining the traffic in the urban outskirts of Menton. The end of the Route! I had no clear idea of what I would do when I got to the Côte d'Azure. In fact I had no idea at all, so I simply carried on until a final road junction demanded a 'left or right?' decision.

On the front at Menton

I chose left and after a brief moment of hesitation was almost physically dragged off the bike by an enthusiastic diner at one of the parasol-shaded restaurants which line the promenade. I felt a bit awkward, rather 'on show', but we chatted amicably, photographs were taken and I took in the scene. The restaurants were on the land side of the road and their open-air tables on the sea side. I don't know if the waiters get formal danger money for dodging the traffic while balancing great trays of food and drink, but I hope the tips are generous. The whole performance was rather like an adaptation of that old computer game which I believe was called *Logger*. My memory is a bit hazy, but it involved crossing a river by jumping on the backs of crocodiles. This was very similar, but involved predicting the speed of cars and finding the gaps with 100-percent accuracy. They are good at it. I was there for about twenty minutes and didn't see a single dead waiter!

Eventually, I motored off into the centre of Menton. I was not greatly attracted by it, the general atmosphere striking me as being a bit like Debenhams at summer-sale time. I hadn't seen any hotels which seemed particularly biker-friendly, or even biker-appropriate at all, so I rode on in the direction of Monaco and Nice. Bearing in mind that it was now mid-afternoon, this may not have been the smartest choice and by the time I reached the Principality, the traffic had achieved critical intensity. *H* is not at home in heavy traffic, but we acquitted ourselves fairly well considering that every time I left a single space between *H* and the Maserati we were following, it would be filled instantly by a large motorcycle and several scooters. It was also very warm and I spent a hectic time whirling around trying to find my way down to the harbour area. We got there eventually, but not before I had passed the Rolls Royce and Bentley tank showrooms twice and been scowled at several times for stopping for pedestrians at crossings. The unnerving thing was that I got scowls from both drivers alongside and the bloody pedestrians. I could have got the distinct feeling that in Monaco/Monte Carlo the vintage bike rider is pretty closely related to vermin, had it not been for the wide grins from a couple of police officers.

This is the point at which I drop into outrageous name-dropping mode and brag about my first visit to Monaco, more than fifty years ago. I was a member of the Mintex service crew at the Rally. On the night of the Rally Ball three or four of us were at a loose end because naturally enough that was a black-tie, no-proles-invited sort of do. We ended up at a little four-lane bowling alley near the centre of town. Only one other lane was in use and we started to get going in ours. The other bowlers looked familiar and soon the penny dropped: we were sharing with Prince Rainier and Princess Grace, who were accompanied by the dancer Gene Kelly. A few minutes later Aristotle Onassis and Maria Callas dropped in to watch. They were all very good and didn't disturb us at all.

Back to my ride on *H*. Eventually I got to the harbour and stopped at the bronze statue of Fangio with his Mercedes at Rascasse corner. We were on the circuit! Phew. *H* went onto her stand and with great relief I took off my sweaty helmet. I was soon surrounded by a group of visitors, mainly British, who were delighted by *H* and together we basked in five minutes of fame while *H* released a drip or two of oil alongside Monaco's otherwise pristine zebra crossing.

On my journey I was asked many questions about *H*. Usually they were perfectly reasonable: 'How many CCs? How fast? How old? How many gears? ... and so on. I enjoy these and have learned to answer in my versions of various European languages. I thought it was quite revealing that here, in Monaco, was the only occasion when I was asked what she was *worth*. I gave a vague 'several thousands, but she's not for sale' reply, thinking that I couldn't enjoy travelling more if I had been in one of those monolithic Rolls Royces or the open-top Maserati.

After photographing Fangio and *H* together, I eyed the crowds, took a deep breath and set off to tackle a lap of the GP circuit. I think it would have been rude not at least to have a go. It was surprisingly tricky because on a slow machine such as *H* it is essential to be in the correct lane all the time, something which is not a consideration for the Lewis Hamiltons of this world when the roads are closed. I learned several things, including just how steep that climb is up from behind the pits; that at racing speeds it must be an act of blind faith to hit the appropriate exit from Casino Square; that the descent to the Tunnel in thick traffic is absolutely as much as *H*'s brakes can cope with, and that the Tunnel itself is noisier and more frightening than I had bargained for! Anyway we managed it and the return to Rascasse was sweet indeed.

After that I had had enough of the rich life of this gilded corner of the Riviera and longed to be up in the quieter hills again. I followed the signs for Nice until in the outskirts I spotted the turn-off to the village of La Turbie and once more poor old *H* found herself being asked to tackle a long stiff climb, a climb which has a rather macabre fame because in 1903 the Count Zborowski met his end at one of the first corners here.

The timed hill-climb to La Turbie was one of the earliest regular motoring events and a highlight of the social calendar on the Riviera more than a century ago. I was interested to see what the road is like today and to try and imagine how it would have been to drive a sporting car up it on the unpaved roads of the early Edwardian era. It also took me away from the heat and clamour of the coast and back in the general direction of the Route des Grandes Alpes again.

The sign reads 'Road Narrow and Dangerous'. This was not an understatement.

It is about 10 miles to the village, and substantial parts of the climb are steeper than 1 in 10, so it is not an insignificant run. Once through it, I got the map out to find a way through the Alpes Maritimes which would take me back onto the Route north-east of Sospel. Much easier said than done! I seemed to be in an endless maze of tiny dangerous roads – many of them single-track with grass down the middle – I know they were dangerous because there were official signs to tell me so. I would not argue with the authorities on that, and the riding was tougher than on many of the high cols. We went via Pelle and planned to stop at the next significant place I could find: L'Escarene. By this time it was evening after a long and fairly challenging day in the saddle. It is fair to say that I was pretty well banking on finding a bed in L'Escarene, so it came as an acute disappointment to discover that the town had been taken over in its entirety by a car rally and that every room was long gone. Soddit. In the shop I was advised to try Contes, back towards Nice. Huh, just what I needed, but no other option. I was deep in the mountains just before sunset, on a motorcycle without lights, so set off towards Contes at once. It seemed to take ages to get there, but probably wasn't more than a quarter of an hour before I reached the town sign and stopped to work out where the centre was. In the end it didn't matter because there was a 'Hotel' sign showing through the trees a hundred metres away and soon I was booked into a slightly strange, but serviceable establishment called *Les Tchitchou'S Night* (sic). I have not managed to translate that with any accuracy. There was a brief period of high drama as my request to park *H* in the large area behind the building rather than on the busy narrow pavement in front led to a protracted session of theatrical negotiation which took my limited command of French to its outer limits, but eventually she was tucked up safely just as the sun disappeared behind the mountains.

The hotel had a good restaurant with a semi-oriental menu. I enjoyed a huge crab and prawn starter and then set about chicken satay and rice. I am possibly being over-sensitive, but I think I detected a slight flicker of disappointment on behalf of the waiter when I turned out to be pretty competent with chopsticks as a result of visits to Japan long ago. Dessert was not up to the standard of the rest: profiteroles which had an unusually high specific gravity, but I was full by then anyway. Not much later, sleep came easily.

Mileage for the day: I reckon about 120miles/190km.
They were tough miles and it felt like a lot more...

Chapter 10

Count Zborowski, La Turbie and Chitty-chitty-bang-bang

I suspect that I am not alone in being able, vaguely, to associate the name 'Zborowski' with giant early racing cars and even sudden death, but the details are sadly lacking. I rummaged through my collection of motoring books and skipped like a flat stone over the surface of the internet to fill in a few details and here they are:

The Count Zborowski, who met his death at one of the early corners of the La Turbie time trial on April Fools' day in 1903, was an American and familiarly known as Eliot. He made his own fortune in real estate and then married into the fabulously wealthy Astor family. To put it mildly, he was 'comfortable' by any standards. He obtained his title in Poland and spent most of his time between the Riviera and England, where he had a country estate. He died at the wheel of a 60hp German Daimler, probably purchased from the Nice dealer, Emil Jellinek, whose daughter Mercedes was to be the inspiration for the name of the marque which lives to this day. It appears that he lost control because when swinging into the corner a cuff-link hooked onto the manual throttle lever at the centre of the steering column. He was only 45 when he died. His chauffeur was riding with him, as was quite normal in the early days of racing, and also received fatal injury.

So what is the connection with Chitty-chitty-bang-bang? Well, the Count's young son, Louis, was naturally his heir and lived with his mother at her extensive estate, Higham Place, in Kent. She died young and just after the Great War Louis found himself to be one of the wealthiest teenagers in the world. He had the resources to indulge in his mechanical passion and in 1921 commissioned a car to race at Brooklands. This was no half-hearted effort: it had a 23-litre 6-cylinder Maybach Zeppelin engine in a modified Mercedes chassis. It became known as 'Chitty-bang-bang'. It has been suggested that this was because of the rattle of its exposed valve-gear in counterpoint to its booming exhaust, but I prefer the explanation that it derives from a bawdy wartime song! Three further 'Chittys' were to follow, culminating in the Higham Special. This had a 27-litre V12 American Liberty engine. It was to gain further fame and finally, notoriety, in the hands of Parry Thomas, who exceeded 170mph before dying in it at Pendine Sands in 1927.

The performance of these aero-engined giants exceeded the durability of the tyres of the day. Those who lapped bumpy Brooklands in them at 120+ mph have my undying admiration. I wish I could have seen them in their heydays.

Young Louis survived his giant cars, only to die at the wheel of a 2-litre Mercedes racer at Monza in 1924.

Ian Fleming subsequently pinched the 'Chitty' name for his children's book, producing a charming story, but managing to lose the raw power and courage embodied in the originals.

The Model H Triumph I ride, is one of around 30.000 produced for military use. After the Armistice, railway wagonloads of them were brought back from France to the Coventry factory where they were reconditioned and sold to private owners after the Great War. It is not at all fanciful to imagine that virtually identical bikes would have been ridden to Brooklands and parked against the fencing on the very days that Louis Zborowski 's giant car was competing there. I like to think that my old bike provides a direct link to those dangerous yet strangely innocent days of motor sport 90-odd years ago. For me, *H* is part-motorbike, part time-machine.

Chapter 11

A break in the proceedings

Saturday 15 September

I awoke to a fine morning, breakfasted and then filled up in Contes at a garage conveniently near the hotel. Then it was across the river to the D 815 for the Col de Chateauneuf. Only 626m (2054ft), but still almost 1500ft of tough climbing – not many ascents like that to start a day in England.

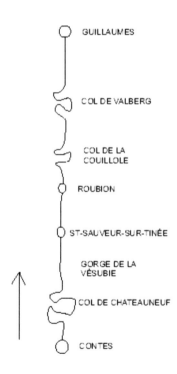

Once over the Chateauneuf we carried on down to the D2205, a main road up the valley of the Tinée. The sun was doing nicely and so was *H* and we bowled along in fine style on the smooth surface. Her engine was running right in the sweet spot, so we were making a steady 38mph towards the next big challenge, the Col de la Couillole and the nearby mountain village of Roubion. Now I had not found myself singing very much on this trip compared with my journeys in Britain, because the concentration demanded by the tough mountain roads kept me busy enough, but the D2205 was routine stuff and *Simon Smith* resurfaced in my consciousness. After about my third chorus of 'I may go out tomorrow if I can borrow a coat to wear' the commotion from the machinery came to an abrupt halt. I whipped the clutch in and coasted to a stop. At such a time it is good to apply a systematic and analytical approach to pinpointing the fault. If only ...

Anyway, I did my best and actually remembered to check the obvious:

a) Is the plug-lead still connected? *It was*
b) Fuel? *Yes, tank half full and tap open*
c) Compression? *Swing kick starter and meet a reassuring amount of resistance. Good*
d) Is there a spark?

At this stage I realised that this may be more than a two-minute job and that the direct sun was pretty damn hot, so I pushed *H* under a little tree by a works' entrance on a small industrial estate and got the tools out. I took the plug out, laid it on the engine and swung the kickstart. There was a lovely blue spark just like the instruction books describe. Mr Bosch's splendid hundred-year-old magneto was still delivering the goods, so no room for improvement there – assuming, of course, that it was occurring at the correct moment. I thought that the odds were in favour of that because of the undramatic way the motor had stopped. On the one occasion I have experienced the timing slipping, it was after a savage backfire when starting up.

Here is a handy tip for the novice: A little caution in positioning the plug is a good thing when laying it on the engine to check for a spark. Carelessness here has resulted in many a bike bursting into flames. All you need to do to get a good blaze going is to kick the engine over several times on a wide throttle opening while tickling the carburettor to make sure that fuel shortage isn't the problem. When it still refuses to start, remove the plug and place it *very close* to the hole it came out of. One more good kick and whoof! The super-rich mixture expelled from the cylinder will ignite, followed by the agglomeration of oil and grease that the years have allowed to build up under the tank and around the engine. The whole lot will get going in no time and only if you kept your head well back will you have preserved your eyebrows.

I tried another plug, because that is what motorcyclists do when they are starting to run out of ideas. Motors came and went up the little lane, but nobody showed the slightest interest in my presence. The change of plug made no difference, so the next thing was to check the fuel flow through the carburettor. Bingo! There wasn't any. I whipped the top off the float bowl and the float and needle came out with it. I will spare you the details, but these are parts which are designed to work together in harmony but exist independently. Their purpose is to regulate the supply of petrol, which requires the needle to move up and down as the float moves. My needle had just moved up and jammed, cutting off all fuel. This is pretty unusual and I suspect that if the D2205 had not such a smooth surface, agitation and gravity would have prevented it. Anyway, I just cleaned everything up and re-seated the needle as best I could by shaping it with the file on my Leatherman and then grinding it in with a little road dust and all was well. I like that bit about using road dust – it has such a ring of the pioneer about it!

After a few more miles on the main road we got back onto the official Route des Grande Alpes near San Sauveur, where I had stayed overnight before the final day's run down to the coast. The Route north offers two choices here: to the east it follows the valley of the Tinée, which would have taken us back over the Cime de la Bonette to Jausiers. As I had done that on the way down, I proposed to return up the west route, via Guillaumes and the Col de la Cayolle to an overnight stop in Barcelonette. This apparently flawless plan started off very well. The scenery was superb and the weather perfect. I stopped at a roundabout to check the map and was immediately adopted by a very helpful biker who insisted on escorting me a couple of miles out of his way to direct me to the Roubion turning. During our route discussions he observed that my choice would take me over the Col de la Cayolle. *Oui* I agreed, and he responded with a long look at *H* and sucked-in cheeks. I explained that we had climbed a few tough passes, such as the Galibier and the Bonette, but his cheeks remained sucked-in.

Grandes Alpes

Roubion is the ultimate dream mediaeval village, apparently nailed to precipices and approached via a splendid serpentine road which allows it to be appreciated from different directions as you climb. In practical terms I suspect that it is probably preferable to *visit* Roubion rather than to live there all year round as access must be challenging for much of the time.

It was a really hard climb and *H* was feeling the heat. I pumped extra oil to help the old dear. My right leg spent much of the time off the footrest and waving in the breeze in an effort to avoid the flesh of my calf being barbecued by radiant heat from the exhaust valve. Once or twice I was struck by an optical illusion which made the road look as if it was descending when it was still going upwards. This could be so convincing that I was conned into changing up a gear before learning the truth. About a kilometre before the village we overtook a lone female cyclist of mature aspect labouring up the final hairpins while loaded down with panniers and camping gear. It looked like a heroic effort to me.

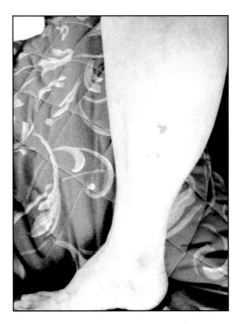

The engine started to fry my calf. Those are burns, not varicose veins!

I turned right into the village and pulled up at the first cafe displaying signs of activity. I attempted to tuck *H* tidily away on her stand at the back of a tiny car-park but the proprietor would have none of it. I thought I had somehow offended him, but no, he was welcoming us and wanted *H* to flaunt herself in full view of the public! Soon I was sitting down to a plate of savoury crêpes and an Orangina. Other customers were making a fuss of *H* when the heroic lady cyclist ground slowly past us. Nobody gave her a glance; it is an unfair world.

When turning into the village I noticed that the other half of the signpost pointed to what I assumed to be the dreaded Col de la Cayolle, a distance of only 1.3km, or something like that. Thinking that I had somehow made a spectacular map-reading error a long way back down the road and that although moderately ferocious, if there was a mere kilometre or so to go, the monster was not greatly to be feared, I set out from the cafe with a light heart. It was a mistake any idiot could make. The pass just beyond Roubion is the Col de la *Couillole* (1678m/5505ft). The *Col de la Cayolle* is a long way further on and a very different matter at 2326m/7630ft!

We motored on through the village of Beuil, taking it easy as usual on the descents and then made the easy ascent of the Col de Valberg 1673m/5489ft. This is a ski area and the pass is one of the mildest of the whole Route, although its frequent inclusion in the Tour de France has given it a cachet undeserved in comparison with such as the Galibier.

I was pleased that we were making really good time and Barcelonette before nightfall was becoming a distinct possibility. On the way down from Valberg I detected an occasional slight ticking from the region of the rear wheel. I stopped to give it a quick coat of looking-at, but couldn't see anything wrong. Soon I was entering the little town of Guillaumes. Imagine,it was mid afternoon with the sun illuminating the monthly market, held in the main street. Well, pretty well the *only* street. Thronged would be a good word for it. The stalls were all busy and family groups spilled all over the road. Mustering all available dignity, *H* and I chugged slowly from one end to the other, our passage attracting considerable attention. I quite fancied stopping for a drink, but the whole place looked so busy that we just kept going. Soon the buildings began to peter out and after a couple of bends which took us past the impressively named *Garage des Grandes Alpes* we were in the countryside again with *H* happily flying along in top gear. It didn't last. With astonishing abruptness and a loud squawk the brake pedal attacked the toe of my left boot. We stopped. The brake block, which acts on the same surface of the large pulley-rim on the back wheel as the drive belt, had jammed, in turn driving its operating rod forwards and forcing the pedal up-and-over. Further investigation revealed that the block had jammed because the pulley-rim itself had split. Indeed, it was entitled to jam. My toe had become the unfortunate final link in this simple chain of mechanical cause-and-effect. I gingerly straightened the rod and pulled the pedal back into position. Unfortunately, as soon as I tried to move the bike at all, the block jammed again. I had to resort to lashing it clear with a cable-tie before riding back into Guillaumes on an almost entirely brakeless machine. At this stage I clearly knew I had a problem, but was not entirely aware of the scale of it and imagined that ten minutes work with a tig-welder may do the trick. One thing was certain: I would not be attempting the Col de la Cayolle today. I rode gingerly back towards the town, noting en route that the Garage des Grandes Alpes, the most obvious source of emergency welding tackle, was indeed closed.

After all, it was Saturday afternoon; I did not bear the owner any malice.

I found a hotel in the main street and booked in without delay. *H* was wheeled into the yard at the back, downwind of a couple of large fully-loaded wheelie-bins which were throbbing gently in the afternoon sun. I went round to the front where it was less fragrant, settled at a table under a parasol and ordered a beer while considering my options. The mood in the bar was jolly. It was full of stallholders bent on spending some of the day's profits and after another beer or two my position didn't feel too bad either. There were, I reflected, worse places to be stranded. That was before I had become intimately acquainted with the menu. Tomorrow was Sunday, which the rural French still respect as a day more-or-less of rest, so I didn't expect any welding to be available anywhere until Monday. And if repair should prove to be impossible, I would simply travel back to Les Gets by public transport, collect my van and drive back to retrieve *H*. Not exactly the perfect finale to my adventure, I admit, but what the hell – I had travelled the Grande Alpes one way at least, and I would have to be content with that. Before going to bed I went to have a really good look at *H*. Any faint hope I had harboured that a magical repair with superglue and gaffer tape would take us both back over several more mountain passes was quickly dispelled. Removing the belt revealed that the split in the pulley-rim was far worse than I had dreamt possible. There were several radial cracks in the wall of the rim and a long split at the bottom of the vee for at least a third of the circumference. In the trade that is known as *totally knackered.*

I phoned Ian Jennings back in England, with whom I had been keeping in touch, to let him know that the trip had come to a grinding halt. After a bit of discussion he convinced me that I should at least try to get the rim bodged-up and finish the run if at all possible. I reflected that the logic was inescapable – there was little to lose and everything to gain – and anyway, it would make a better story!

One way or another it had been a full day. I went to bed.

75miles/120km approx

Chapter 12

Long hot Sunday

This chapter can be skipped by those readers who: A) are easily bored: B) have no technical interest whatever: C) are of a nervous disposition.

Apart from a mild bout of competitive bell-ringing at an earlier hour than was strictly necessary in my opinion, there was little promise of excitement in Guillaumes on Sunday morning. I felt as if I was suspended by the day, condemned to inactivity. Then, when I thought about it, the action to take was obvious: get the belt-rim off the wheel in the hope that it could be welded-up on Monday. If it could, fine. If not, at least I would have tried and would just have to make my way back to my van at Les Gets by fair means or foul and then return for *H*. I would lose nothing by dismantling the rim because the bike was incapacitated anyway. There was a distant third option, which was to phone to England for a serviceable rim to be sent out to me, a procedure which would obviously take time and by now, after only one night, I was beginning to realise that my affection for the hotel was unlikely to persist indefinitely.

At this point the astute reader may well be thinking 'Surely he had some sort of recovery insurance; why not just ring up and be collected?' Well, yes, I did, but somehow using it would have been entirely at odds with the spirit in which I approach my long-ish rides. A trip like this is an exercise in self-sufficiency and arriving back home courtesy of Carole Nash Insurance or the RAC would have felt like failure bordering on humiliation. Perversely, if I was just out for the day and broke down seriously within 20 or 30 miles of home, I wouldn't think twice about using a recovery service. Logical? Perhaps not, but it is the way I am.

I set to work on *H* in the yard beside the refuse bins, which in the cool of the morning had not yet developed their full flavour. With the bike on the stand it was a straightforward job to detach the belt completely, slacken two nuts and free the wheel from the fork. Getting the wheel out of the frame from beneath the mudguard requires a little practice. At first sight it is impossible, but if you know the knack it is dead easy. Keeping the bike on its stand, you position yourself on the left of it and pull the saddle towards you until it all balances against your hips on the left leg of the stand. Now reach over to roll the wheel out diagonally from the right. It took me some time to learn to do this easily, but I pass on the knowledge gratis.

With the wheel out, the next stage was to unscrew the tyre valve and remove tyre and tube, which is very easy with the beaded-edge type of tyre. Detaching the belt-rim was rather more tedious as it is secured with 20 very short spokes which had probably been in use since 1918 and the nipples were all well worn. In theory the best way to undo these would have been with a screwdriver from the tyre-side of the rim, but the slots were so mangled that it was impossible. The alternative was to turn the spoke-nipples with my small adjustable spanner or, once they had been loosened a bit, the pliers on my Leatherman tool. All very tedious because I could achieve only a quarter-turn a go. By the time I had removed the lot and had the belt-rim free in my hand, the sun had reached the bins.

Now close inspection revealed the true extent of the damage and it didn't get any better. The rim was fatigued almost to death. It was broken for at least a third of its circumference and there were several other minor splits. Obviously it had taken more stick than was reasonable, particularly during the spell in the traffic of Monaco. I must admit that quick repair with a bit of welding now seemed an exotic desire. I washed it with petrol, so that it looked as good as it was going to look and smelt a damn sight better than the bins.

At first glance the rim appears ok, but look closely
and you'll see the extent of the splits

As the day progressed the tables in front of the hotel began to fill with patrons and the bar became steadily more animated. I had little use for either as the effects of the very good French breakfast had not yet fully worn off, so I sought other diversions. There was only one, a child's bicycle with a tragically flat tyre which seemed to have spent some time keeping the bins company. I was fully pumped-up in wheel and tyre removal and so it seemed too good an opportunity to miss. Moving effortlessly into hero mode and guessing that only one of the cycle patches I had in *H*'s toolbox would be required to fix it and thus bring years of gratitude from a small child, I sought out someone who appeared to be a female member of the family loosely in command of the hotel and asked if she would like me to repair it. About a minute after receiving an affirmative reply I had the tyre off and was inspecting the tube. It appeared unblemished, so I inflated it. After a short time throbbing in the sun alongside the bins, it had lost pressure. I pumped it up again and rushed round to the front of the hotel and into the toilet adjacent to the bar where there was an intriguing double hand-basin of a pattern probably last fashionable when *H* was new. Immersing the tube produced a satisfying stream of tell-tale bubbles revealing the source of the leak which I marked by pressing it with my thumb. It was then a simple matter to stick on a patch and re-inflate it. I returned to the curious double sink and tested it again. More bubbles, another patch. This was repeated until I had exhausted all my patches in spite of cutting the last couple in half. I am a slow learner, but I had not encountered a truly age-perforated tube before. Unable to do more, I put the cover back on and hoped it would stay in shape until just after I left, at least.

All this to-ing and fro-ing to the sink had, as they say, an upside, in that on one trip I got into conversation with Christophe, a young man enjoying a beer outside in the sun. He turned out to be an enthusiast for old machines and used a lovely 1964 Peugeot forward-control van for everyday transport. I later joined him and he showed me where there was a *ferronnerie* – a metalworker's yard – and, a little further on, the garage I had seen earlier. The owner, he told me, liked vintage bikes and he thought he owned one. We peered through the windows and I could make out the rear of a very old motorcycle buried in the spidery depths. I took this as an encouraging omen.

Christophe was travelling to Grenoble later in the day and he offered me and *H* a lift there, as it would offer better prospects of public transport onwards to where my van was parked. However, I decided to try my luck with getting repairs done where I was. I felt that the combined resources of the metalworker and the garage might just deliver the goods and I really wanted to complete the ride on *H* if I possibly could.

By mid-afternoon I had exhausted the diversions Guillaumes had to offer, so followed the example of several of the locals and relaxed at a table in an open-air bar to take in the scene. I am diverted by the steady flow of motorcycles going past: big BMWs are popular, but there is also a large number of the relatively new breed of touring scooters – the Suzuki Bergman and its ilk. A cut-down Buell, all snort and snarl, is followed by a smooth Honda Pan European. The Buell reminds me of a bull-terrier, and the Honda, a saluki. The sky is perfectly clear and I think I am allowed to call it *azure* without sounding unduly poetic in this context. It contrasts perfectly with the ochre Roman tiles of the little town's roofs and all the expected picturesque accessories, green shutters, ruins on the hills and a slow cat that strolls past from time to time. Just after my second coffee, the one I decided to accompany with a glass of genepi, the liqueur of the Grandes Alpes, a very new-looking Harley Davidson had pulled up in a parking bay by the hotel. It needed all of it. It is a bright shiny blue Electra Glide

98

adorned with accessories enough to equip a small town. The light brown passenger accommodation looks like an advertisement for World of Leather. I contemplate its mass and wonder how one would cope with a rear-wheel puncture. In the wet... At night. It is probably better not to dwell on it. Mysteriously, I had not noticed the Harley's arrival – I guess I must have been watching the cat at the time.

It was a different story an hour later when it left. The exhaust system had obviously been engineered for full 'look at me' effect and the whole town knew it was leaving. Somehow the raw staccato blast seemed inappropriate for the chromium opulence of the rest of it, even if it was still delivered with that asymmetric Harley rhythm. I felt that a burble rather than a string of individual thunderclaps would have suited the sheer opulence of the machine better.

I was happy to linger outside for as long as I could remain entertained, because I had again run out of reading material. A neighbour was presented with a vast bowl of ice-cream. He was grandfatherly and I assumed he was going to serve it out into individual portions and waited to watch the rest of the family join him – I expected three at least, probably four – and none would have gone short. He scoffed the lot, single handed. It was no mystery why he was almost spherical and walked only with the aid of a stick.

The time passed agreeably, with the aid of a phone call from my son Matthew who was also in the mountains, but the Bavarian ones. He had just done rather well in a paragliding competition and shared that along with lots of other family news. How the mobile phone has facilitated relationships. We now lead lives that Buck Rogers would have found fanciful.

My supply of reading matter in English having become exhausted once more, I resorted to a collection of French motor and motorcycle magazines which were left out in the hotel as one of the meagre comforts for guests. Consequently, my French conversation improved steadily as long as long as I was able to steer the subject towards motoring . Some of the magazines dealt exclusively with classic cars. I am often amused to see how vehicles of 30 or 40 and more years ago which I owned briefly and was more than happy to see the back of, have survived to become 'collectable'. The Renault 14 sticks in my memory as being a particularly unpleasant machine which rusted away faster than the MG 1100 which preceded it, and that's saying something. I spent some time on the accessory pages and was delighted to come across a *bougie de gonflage* on offer. I knew that a bougie was a spark-plug and that gonflage was inflation, but it took a bit of time for me to dredge the least-visited parts of my memory to recall that this was a gadget which used the car's engine to pump up tyres by screwing it into a sparking-plug hole. I remember that the advertisements for it in Motor Sport long ago stressed that it pumped only fresh air and not petrol fumes. Naturally it also depended on there being an engine with enough cylinders for it not to miss one when tyre-inflation duties were called for. I forget what this was called in English, but it will always be a *bougie de gonflage* to me from now on.

With this enforced inactivity I began to take more notice of my hotel and the rather freestyle system of management which was in use. It was largely based on the model established by Basil Fawlty, with several subtle Gallic adaptations. I do not propose to go into great detail, but let me put it this way: the breakfasts were great but it was downhill from there on. There seemed to be plenty of personnel, but none of them showed any significant sense of organisation or responsibility, merely freewheeling from one cigarette break to the next. Fag breaks played a prominent part in the passage of time here. I need not have worried about the security of my belongings in the room because as far as I could tell nobody entered it from the time I booked in until the day I left. If they did, they certainly didn't make the bed ...

Miles: nil

Chapter 13
The Monday of reckoning

Today I would find out. Could the rim be repaired or would I be thumbing lifts back to my van a couple of hundred hilly kilometres or more to the North? Rim in hand, I walked down the main street to the ferronnerie. It was a father-and-son business specialising in gates and garage doors, but had the air of being able to take on anything where a bit of welding was involved. I showed them my sad exhibit and was not really surprised when, after a short, but reasoned discussion they came to the conclusion that there simply was not sufficient thickness of metal to join anything to. This was kindly explained with a suitable garniture of shrugs and sucked-in cheeks and I left them, feeling that they would have helped if they could. It did not do a lot for my confidence and left me with just the Garage des Grandes Alpes to try. It was a few hundred metres further out of town.

The scene of H's redemption

Max, the garage patron, gave me a good listening to. With my hit-and-miss French this cannot have been easy for him as he obviously had his hands full with jobs for the day, but he is a true gentleman. He grasped the problem instantly, asked a couple of questions about the amount of clearance around the rim when it was on the bike and started bending a small strip of metal which had been lying on the bench. After a few minutes with vice and hammer he offered it up, made a few tweaks and suggested that if many such pieces were fitted around the rim, it might hold. I had been imagining a few long shallow strips welded or brazed along the base of the rim. His solution was much more likely to succeed: many separate reinforcing plates bent to the outside section of the vee and joined on radially over it. Hard to describe, but the picture should give a better idea. I had not considered this approach at all, but could see that although clumsy at first sight, it stood the best chance of working.

A problem soon emerged in that Max had only enough scrap to make one more piece and the job would need about a dozen. He suggested I go to the *ferronnerie* and see if they had anything suitable. I walked back there, past some allotments where giant squashes were being harvested, and, after a little explanation, was given a number of suitable metal-strip off-cuts. They would accept no payment and I sensed that they didn't give a lot for my chances of success either. Bearing in mind that the metal pieces were a gift it would have been churlish to point out that they were not all of the same width or thickness, which would complicate the job slightly.

Back at the garage Max charmingly but firmly made it clear that I was on my own now as he was busy on customers' cars, but that I had the free run of the bench and its vices. Fair enough.

It was up to me to make 10 or 11 copies of his prototype, as close as I could get them. The vices had seen life and lots of it, to put it mildly, but I couldn't have managed without them. There was also a small guillotine which was just up to cutting the metal, so at least no hacksawing was involved. It must have taken me the best part of two hours and ingenious use of vice, spacers, hammer and a giant Mole wrench to get the job done. Just as Max finished a service on his customer's car I proudly lined up my morning's work on the bench for his inspection. He approved. Now it was a matter of attaching them to the rim. He produced a spot welder which I had not noticed before. If I had seen it, I would probably not have been able to identify it with any confidence because it was not like any spot-welder I had ever come across, but then, my familiarity with garage equipment doesn't go back much before 1950. It had acquired a patina of antiquity and blended in well with the bench and vices. Max put it in the centre of the floor and plugged it in via a sinister length of oily black cable as thick as my finger. He then seized the rim, clamped one of the reinforcements to it with the aforementioned Moles and with uncanny accuracy brought the electrodes together on the job. They hissed and fizzed unenthusiastically, but no weld resulted. He inspected the job again and repeated the action. This time something really did happen: with a bang and a flash all the lights went out, the radio fell silent and the compressor ground to a halt. Wiggling plugs and inspecting fuses had zero effect, but Max was unfazed. Abandoning the welder he produced pop-rivets, a small power drill and a 12volt car battery. Sorted! After securing one end of each of the pieces with a couple of pop-rivets he declared lunchtime and I walked back into town. At the house where the slow cat seemed to live there was a dead snake on the doormat. Perhaps the cat is not really so slow after all.

Things were falling into place gradually. At a little supermarket I bought some washing-up liquid and a brush to get my hands halfway clean again. I also used it to give the belt a good scrub as I felt the need to display some optimism that *H* and I would eventually leave under our own steam. Soon enough it was time to wander up the road again, past the squash harvesters and to the garage. Max had managed to restore electric power, but wasn't going to chance his luck with spot-welding again. He declared that the other ends of the reinforcements would be bronze-welded in place. Out came the oxy/acetylene bottles and the search for brazing rod started. It was unfortunate that he was able to find only a short stub, not a couple of inches long. Insufficient by any standard. Naturally, Max was not stuck completely. "You may be able to get some at the *ferronnerie*" he suggested. I knew the way by now. When I got there it seemed touch and go because a lot of rummaging was needed before they located the correct rods. Their entire stock was three, which I was happy to buy before walking back past the site of the squash harvest which the heat of the afternoon seemed to have arrested. There were large padlocks on the allotment gates, I noted, suggesting that perhaps life in Guillaumes was not always as idyllic and crime-free as one may have hoped.

Refreshed by the sight of full lengths of rod, there was no holding Max. The joints were made at great speed and it never even looked as if there was any risk of burning holes in the flimsy metal of the rim. If I'd been doing it there would have been a couple, for sure – I'm years out of practice with a welding torch.

Max and the patched-up rim. Couldn't have achieved it without him!

The end product looked pretty sad, I have to admit, with its new crude additions, pocked with pop-rivets and the remaining paint extensively scorched by the torch, but it felt strong. After paying Max the modest fee he requested, I walked the kilometre back to the hotel where *H* was waiting by the bins, and settled down to a wheel reassembly session. It went well, aided by unearthing my set of magneto spanners, a dainty little thing formed like a miniature fan. I had sought it earlier, but it wasn't in the toolbox where I expected it to be and so thought I must have forgotten to pack it. One of its spanners fitted the spoke-nipples perfectly. I wished I had found it yesterday!

I tightened the rim onto the wheel as best I could, then fitted it all into the bike so I could turn it easily and check how true it was running. It wasn't running true at all, but with a fair amount of strategic spoke tightening and slackening I got it somewhere near. It also needed some bold bending with mole grips and tyre lever to get the sides of the belt channel parallel-ish. After a sweaty hour surrounded by the aroma of the bins I was feeling quite pleased with myself. I couldn't wait to fit the tyre again, but had to because there was another snag. All the heating, bending, hitting and tweaking had made the rim 'grow' slightly and now the ends of the little spokes were sticking out in places and would inevitably chafe the tyre from inside if I left them like that. I tried filing one down with my Leatherman tool, but soon gave up when it became clear that I would need all night. There was only one thing for it: back to Max's garage for a short session with the abrasive wheel – I had seen one there. I did not enjoy the two-kilometre round trip at all. It was one thing to do it with the rim on its own, but now I had to carry the complete wheel. It's not a great weight, but it makes an awkward load; quite enough on a warm afternoon, especially as it has to be held just away from the body a bit to keep the spindle ends clear of the legs. Fortunately, when I reached the garage the grinder made short work of the spokes. It had been worth the effort.

Tyre fitting was easy but blowing it up with the cycle-type pump I carry seemed to take forever. By the end of the afternoon I had everything together again and it was time for a test run. I got as far as the edge of the pavement before the brake-block grabbed and locked the wheel. Forward motion was impossible and I was aware of a small audience sitting in the cafe, agog to be further entertained by the eccentric Englishman. I stopped the motor and wheeled *H* confidently backwards, trying to look as if that was what I had in mind all the time. I doubt if I convinced anyone. The problem was that although the rim was held together well enough for the belt to drive, it was no longer sufficiently smooth for the much harder brake block to function correctly. It took another session at the bins for a bit of radical spring-bending and block-filing before I got any sense into what is referred to throughout this book as 'the brake', although that is really for reference purposes only and should not suggest that it is in reality a device which can ever be relied on to bring *H* to a halt on demand. At least I stopped it jamming, but I knew that if I stood on it in an emergency, the best I could hope for would probably be a completely locked wheel and the rim terminally wrecked. I test-ran the belt by running the bike in gear on its stand and the drive seemed OK. I left the brake well alone and vowed to avoid its use at all for the rest of the run as far as possible. Gingerly I rode up to Max's for his approval and a quick blast from the airline to top up the rear tyre properly. His working day was almost over and he had time to show me his 1929 Automoto, a popular and good quality French motorcycle from the vintage years. I was also able to buy a half-litre of good thick straight oil from him: SAE60 – rare indeed, but *H* loved it.

On returning to my hotel, I fell into conversation with a Danish tourist who asked me with elaborate politeness if I minded him photographing *H* as it was the first time he'd come across anything like her. Of course, I was delighted. I do like the polite approach, though. Some folk treat us as if we have been provided by the local tourist board as picturesque props!

After my energetic day I was ready for a beer and a meal. The Dane, whose name turned out to be Karsten, recommended the restaurant of a hotel he had found and by now being totally disillusioned with what was on offer where I was staying, I cleaned up and went there for dinner. It was in the only corner of town I had not already explored and was a revelation. If only I had broken down outside *La Renaissance*! Lovely atmosphere and a superb meal of rabbit terrine, grilled trout and apple tart, and I bet it was all sourced locally.

Karsten was attempting to follow one of those insane ultra-endurance events in which the participants run, swim, kayak, climb, cycle and generally suffer exposure, exhaustion and general misery in the pursuit of athletic satisfaction and at the whim of a TV production company. The course is secret and the competitors are supposed to receive no support. It is all surrounded by a curious hush-hush atmosphere. Once I became aware of what was going on in this corner of the Alps I began to notice odd pairs of sinewy folk who looked like thinly disguised sports coaches, lurking among rocks by the roadside. I never got to hear any more about the event and have no idea if the Danish team benefited from Karsten's presence. I expect it will surface at a strange hour on one of the lesser Freeview channels in a year or two. By comparison, riding a 95-year-old motorcycle over foreign mountains feels to me completely rational.

Mileage: 2 kilometres under power and at least 10 kilometres on foot

Chapter 14

Looking after myself

Monday had been a rather energetic day by my standards. A few years ago I had a heart attack which put me in hospital for more than two weeks and left me extremely weak for the following couple of months. I now have a chest full of stents and take a pill or three daily. I also have a very good life. I tried to follow all the advice I was given about diet and exercise and it has worked well. I still go to the *Heartwatch* gym sessions at the local leisure centre twice a week and am sure it is good for me. I felt exhilarated about getting through Monday without any difficulty, but after all, I was only following the British Heart Foundation's advice about being active every day, wasn't I?

The BHF is an excellent charity which I am happy to support. It provides a lot of good advice to people like me, but oh dear, it is not very inspirational. Their *Living with heart failure* booklet has a picture of a dithery-looking old git on the cover, doing a gentle bit of potting. I wanted more than that and have found it in the world of vintage motorcycles. I write this in the hope that others may also discover that heart trouble need not be an excuse to take things easy and start looking for a bungalow. Yes, there certainly are limitations. I know that I am not as strong as I used to be and that I get tired more easily. Those are things you learn to work around pretty quickly. Starting my alpine ride I was interested to see if the reduced oxygen at altitude would give me any problems, but it did not. However, I didn't push my luck and when I parked the bike at the top of a col and saw that it was a 15-minure walk up to a 'vista panoramique', I contented myself with the view from the parking area. Maybe I am being chicken here, as people with heart failure climb Everest. Anyway, my theory is that with any problem such as mine, you can probably do more than you first imagine and I'm more than happy to take a chance on that.

About the only activity of any significance that I have had to give up has been skiing. Much as I loved it, I had to face the reality that I simply no longer had the stamina to get full enjoyment from days on the slopes. I am a little frustrated by this as many ski-lift operators grant free passes to pensioners over 75 and was looking forward to taking advantage of that!

I love being among mountains and throughout my life I have been attracted to sports that have taken me there. Now I am so pleased that I can continue to get a bit of adventure out of them on an old bike.

Chapter 15
Cayolle and beyond

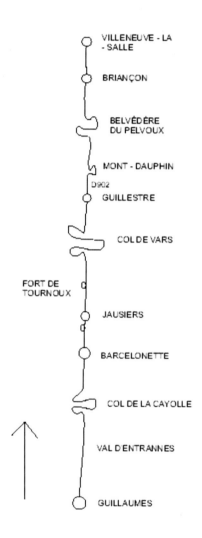

Tuesday September 18

Lying in bed on my final morning in Guillaumes, I made a mental check on the spannerwork I had done yesterday. I thought it was all reasonably sound, but eventually I paused to think about the extra weight I had added to *H*'s rear wheel and to kick myself mentally for not having made any attempt to balance it. As I was loading the bike up after booking out (slightly pointedly not leaving a tip) I thought about what I could do. On the one hand I was really keen to get on the road again; on the other, I didn't want the rim repair to be shaken apart through unbalance. To do a proper job meant taking the belt off and endless fiddling about with I knew not what to balance the wheel. The prospect didn't attract me much. I wanted to get away from the hotel without more mechanicing. In the end I compromised with a typical Whittall bodge. I chose a likely looking open-ended spanner from the toolbag and strapped it to the belt rim with a couple of cable-ties at a point where I estimated its weight would do the most good. We were on the road again!

The balance spanner

H was running beautifully and I wish I could communicate exactly how good it felt to be motoring towards my goal once more on this fresh sunny morning. The Col de la Cayolle and Barcelonette, were on the signposts and the kilometres ticked away. *Simon Smith and the Amazing Dancing Bear* put in a brief appearance, but were soon displaced by another tune from the same period: *Freedom Come, Freedom Go*, which fitted the rhythm of *H*'s 550cc heartbeat better. The belt kept driving, the wheel didn't feel as if it was being shaken to pieces and altogether the world felt pretty damn good.

We went through the village of St Martin d'Entraunes following a couple of gigantic trucks transporting sheep. There is a hairpin bend right in the centre and if I hadn't witnessed it, I would not have given odds on them getting through but the drivers were on top of the job and made it with millimetres to spare. Sheep are big business in the mountains and they were being gathered ready for the big annual sales in October. We came across shepherds at work quite often.

The actual climb of the Col (2326m/7631ft) was as steep as any we had met and the surface quite rough in places. We were chugging up the road, just nicely hanging on in second gear and admiring the views when a big man in a big white crash helmet and a big blue suit on a big Honda pulled alongside and signalled me to stop. It was on a steepish stretch and I struggled to find a half-level spot to park on, but you don't ignore a Gendarme, do you? But it turned out he wasn't a cop, but simply a rather ignorant chump from Toulouse who wanted us to pose for a photo. I took the opportunity to let *H* cool down for a few minutes and as he receded I was able to analyse my thoughts. They amounted to *what a prick*!

It was cold and windy at the top and the parking area was not a particularly good one, so we didn't stop long. As we went over a few bumps on the way out I felt the lever of the valve-lifter rattle against my left glove. That is not something which is supposed to happen, so I suspected that not all was well. Sure enough, it was flapping loose, unconnected to its cable. On a normal motorcycle with brakes, that would have been merely an inconvenience when starting up. On *H* in normal circumstances, where control of speed on descents relies largely on being able to lift the exhaust valve and make the engine work as a pump, it had more significance. On *H* with a crudely patched-up rim which I half expected would disintegrate any minute and so didn't dare to apply the brake to at all, it was a definite challenge. Anyway, we were rolling and I decided to make the best of it until we were down into lesser but warmer altitude. With frequent visits to bottom gear and loads of patience, we made it and were happy eventually to roll along the broad valley road into Barcelonette by lunchtime.

We freewheeled to a stop in Carrefour's supermarket car park and I set about fixing the cable. The nipple had pulled off at the handlebar end. No-one to blame but me because it was a cable I had soldered up. It had served well for years, so I am not sure why it chose the top of a mountain to let go. Anyway, I had a solderless nipple with me and repair should have been easy except ... the cable-end fits completely within the bar and the solderless replacement was too bulky to go in. I checked the cable down on the engine and was relieved to see that the nipple there would fit within the handlebar OK, so I reversed the whole inner cable and fitted the solderless nipple in the oily depths beneath the exhaust valve. Worked fine.

A Carrefour car park is a great place to fix a bike because anything you may need is to hand. A large tuna sandwich and soft drink took care of lunch and a pack of those little connectors with screws in which are sold to join electric wire provided a horde of replacements for the one-and-only spare nipple I had been carrying. An amiable young woman with a scooter chatted for a while and then a couple of German bikers joined me. They approved of *H* and were impressed with the repaired rim. Spotting the tied-on balance-spanner they cried 'Ah, a McGuyver!' such is the reach of decades-old American TV series.

Eventually, I got on the road again, following a not-entirely-instinctive one-way system out of Barcelonette towards Jausiers and the Col du Vars. A treat here is the Fort de Tournoux, a few kilometres on the left after leaving Jausiers. This huge military installation of barracks and fortifications is designed to dominate the trade route over the Alps. The French and the Savoyards found it difficult to agree on control of this and resorted to shooting it out from time to time. Once the French felt they had finally got a grip on it in the late 18th century, they set about fortifying the hillside in a big way and hanging on to it for keeps. Orthodox historians may be a bit picky about how I have explained this, but you get the general idea. It is impressive from the road and if I go there again (hope I do) I will take a day out to explore the Fort in detail.

After the Fort, the road gets progressively more wiggly as it makes its way up the Col du Vars (2108m/6916ft). Although this is a fairly main road, my diary records it as 'very tough'. I had to stop and clean the belt with petrol on the way to stop it slipping. I noted that the views from the top were particularly good and that we got a lot of attention from tourists. By now *H* was getting rather blasé about that.

Descending the Col with the aid of a functioning valve lifter was no problem, but it was a long way, with quite a lot of traffic. The views really were something and we looked down on the roofs of Guillestre for ages before getting into the town and finding the turn-off to the D9024, a little road which would connect us to the Queyras and Durance valleys and eventually to Briançon without having to tackle the Col d'Izoard again. The two valleys are separated by the Belvédère du Pelvoux, a good place for a pause in the journey. You will find there a rather indifferent statue of Edward Whymper, the British Alpine pioneer who made the first ascent of the Matterhorn in 1865, his triumph muted by the loss of four of his companions.

On the climb to the Belvédère we laboured up a series of wide lacets at a steady speed in second gear. Looking up and well ahead I saw a pair of motorcycle gendarmes, one male, one female, observing the traffic generally and *H* in particular. They had placed themselves strategically inside the point of a hairpin, side-by-side, arms behind backs, legs apart. I watched them plot my progress, the note of the Triumph hardly changing as we climbed towards them and swung round the tight bend, taking care not to drift out and obstruct other traffic. I was definitely on their radar! I mentally totted up the myriad small offences I may have been guilty of, particularly the one about having no papers with me. I even had time to think *Oh well, if the worst comes to the worst, at least I won't have to find a hotel tonight.* Sure enough, as we came level with them they turned in unison. 'This is it', I was certain, and prepared to be pulled over. But no. With broad grins they gave me a cheer and a beautifully synchronised double thumbs up!

Elated, we made our way through Briançon in heavy traffic without difficulty – it does help when you know where you are going – and out the other side to the lovely slightly mad Hotel Le Chatelas, at Villeneuve la Salle, on the road to the north of the town. I had not pre-booked, but *H* and I had a wonderful welcome from M Sébastian and his team. I was given the room next to the one I had on the way down. The en-suite facility was equipped with a closet labelled simply *Watermatic.* It lacked the macho brutality of the WATERFLASH ACTANA 700 next door, but functioned well enough. Dinner was excellent.

Approx 95miles /155km

Chapter 16

Reading and writing

It is fair to say that very little forward planning went into my Alpine ride. Virtually none, actually. It was all rather a scramble; I had been demonstrating *H* at the Beamish open-air museum for a couple of days and returned home on Sunday 2 September. My diary for the 3rd and 4th reads 'Did little except work frantically on de-coking *H* and fitting a different set of cams'. De-coking, or to give the process its due dignity *decarbonising*, was once a routine and normal part of running almost any type of motor vehicle. It is a mucky business which involves removing accumulated carbon from the combustion chamber and its immediate surroundings. It's more difficult on bikes of *H*'s era because the cylinder and combustion chamber are cast in one piece, so the lot has to be removed and the carbon chiselled away by poking suitable implements up the bore and through the valve cap spaces. Of course, to get the cylinder out of the frame, the carburettor and exhaust have to come off too. It is a frustrating game and about as congenial as cleaning the oven at a student squat. 'Suitable implements' means blunt scrapers which won't make any impression on the metal under the carbon. By the end of the 1920s, engines had removable cylinder heads and the job was much easier and quicker. *H* needs a de-coke every couple of thousand miles or so. As long as the engine seems to be running happily it is tempting to ignore it until one warm day it begins to cough and rattle. The cause will probably be pre-ignition caused by the accumulated carbon in the region of the exhaust valve glowing and thus exploding the incoming charge too soon, rather than leaving it for the sparking-plug to get on with the job at the right time.

The replacement cams would lift the valves just a little higher than the ones that *H* came with and so should aid her breathing. They were not new, but seemed slightly less worn than the originals. I also fitted one new piston ring and Ian supplied a pair of valve guides. I assembled it all with immense care and it wouldn't go. I had got the valve timing wrong. I have successfully timed many engines over the years, but there's a first for everything. Fortunately Ian was able to put me back on the right lines and by the 5th it was running beautifully, so we went for a test run to the Sun Inn, over a route I often use. It includes the ascent of Norwood Edge, a punishing climb out of Wharfedale. *H* was on top form and I was glad I had made the effort of tuning her up a bit.

On Thursday the 6th I raced around getting correspondence out of the way, putting Euros onto my Eurocard at Thomas Cook, booking a ferry, loading *H* into the van and packing anything I thought I may need.

On Friday I set off to drive down to Dover, there being no space on the Hull ferry. As I was about to leave I realised that I had overlooked reading matter and grabbed a book from my shelves which I hadn't read for at least twenty years. It was a rather yellowed paperback copy of *Nothing By Chance*, by Richard Bach, who is best known for *Jonathan Livingstone Seagull*. I never cared much for *Jonathan Livingstone*, which is too fanciful for me, but Bach is an excellent writer and I have enjoyed his more factual works. In the 1960s he flew around the American Mid-west in a biplane, giving rides and trying to recapture the spirit of the barnstormers of the twenties. *Nothing By Chance* is all about one of those summers and it turned out to be a most appropriate choice. He describes the search for spares for his ancient aircraft and obviously takes the same delight that I do when I stumble across obsolete parts for my bikes. I was particularly impressed when he describes finding a tin of SAE 60 (60 *weight* in USA-speak) oil, the ideal type for the Wright Cyclone radial engine in his 1929 aircraft. By the 1960s that apparently had become almost impossible to find in the USA. Now 50 years later in Europe on my travels I can relate exactly to that as I find it almost impossible to get straight SAE 50, which is *H*'s beverage of choice. Only specialists stock it as most motors built within living memory prefer multigrade oil with detergent additives. I was, therefore, more than impressed when Max at the garage not only had some SAE 60 for his own bike, but was prepared to let me have some of it. With 60 in the oil tank, I wouldn't mind diluting it with 20/50 if I had to.

What's so good about single grade oil? Well, *H*'s oiling arrangements are primitive and there is no form of filter at all. Therefore any carbon, grit or other contaminants stay in the oil for as long as it is splashing around in the engine. Sooner or later solid bits will probably be flung off the flywheels onto the inside of the crankcase and with any luck will stay there. To my mind they will do less harm there than they would have if they were dissolved and stayed in the oil. Also, *H* runs incredibly hot, so a thick lubricant is a good thing. Of course, most of the oil is burned or leaks out, so my concern may well be ill-founded, but I really have managed to convince myself that she runs cooler and keeps compression better on straight 50 than 20/50!

I am a compulsive reader. I begin to panic a bit when I run out of material and I knew the Richard Bach book would not keep me going for long. However, I had no concern because I packed my iPad into the van on leaving England and would be able to download as many books as I wanted whenever I was within reach of a wireless connection. Oh, how I have almost become a slave to technology! Unfortunately I set off on *H* with the iPad still in the van and found myself living off the land as far as English books were concerned. Rural alpine France is a poor source of these.

Chapter 17

Epic day

I left the quaint hotel with a big send-off from Madame Roi, the proprietrice, and Monsieur Sébastian, her Maitre d'. I planned to ride north as far as the Col du Lauteret, which we had met previously after descending the Galibier. This time however, we would follow the western loop of the Route des Grandes Alpes by turning left to Le Verney and on over the Col de la Croix de Fer, which I knew had a bit of a reputation, particularly among pedal cyclists. The weather was rather English, but I was optimistic that it would warm up as the sun climbed over the mountain tops. In this I was not entirely correct and by the time we reached the summit of the Lauteret the cloud was at eye level and I stopped to don my foul-weather coat, which is one of those which Australians use for rounding up kangaroos. I was glad of it, even though it makes *H* look as if she is being ridden by someone clad in a wardrobe. We turned left, signposted *Alpe-D'Huez and Grenoble*.

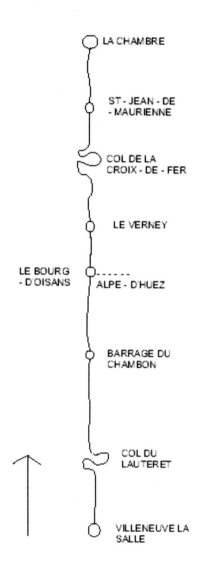

LA CHAMBRE

ST - JEAN - DE
- MAURIENNE

COL DE LA
CROIX - DE - FER

LE VERNEY

LE BOURG
- D'OISANS

ALPE - D'HUEZ

BARRAGE DU
CHAMBON

COL DU
LAUTERET

VILLENEUVE LA
SALLE

Bearing in mind that at this stage I was taking every kilometre as a bonus, this was quite a bold decision. The repaired rear wheel was bearing up well, but I had done only one day on it and still half-expected it to split with every other beat of the exhaust. Sure, I had taken a prod at it once or twice and it seemed sound, but I still thought of it as 'fragile' and tried to treat it as such.

We struck off along the Combe du Malaval, stopping for a coffee and warm-up at Villar d'Arlene, where the chef of Le Faranchin restaurant was captivated by H and our journey. The road was not difficult and the views wonderful all the way: on the left is the reservoir formed by the Barrage du Chambon, while on the right is a waterfall, the *Cascade de la Pisse.* No points for subtlety there, then.

Cascade de la Pisse

The direction is due east for the first 50km or so, then bears north through Le Bourg-d'Oisans, where I had to make a decision. Would I go up the hard climb to Alpe d'Huez or not? It is considered part of the Route. The climb is a tough one but it is a dead end, so we would have had to retrace our way for much of it. I didn't mind climbing but in the near-brakeless state the thought of many hundreds of extra metres of descent did not much appeal. If it had been a sunny day, I probably would have had a go, and if I had been a bit less sensitive about the back wheel I would certainly have tackled it, but I decided against. So it was on through Le Verney and on up to see if there really was an iron cross at the top of the Col de la Croix de Fer!

The seasons were changing now

It was a really long drag in cold and strong wind. There was no doubt that the seasons were changing now. The character of this col differed from most of the others we had tackled. It felt more remote and we didn't see any other vehicles for long periods. The overall climb was interspersed with some short sharp descents followed by equally stiff short climbs. *H*'s engine was producing enough power to cope with these, but eventually one proved too much for the belt, which began to slip. Naturally, this was on a steep narrow bit close to a blind corner and I had a job to find anywhere flat enough for *H* to be put safely on her stand so I could attend to the belt. The only place was on a narrow strip between the tarmac and a drainage ditch. I didn't relish my task, but put vinyl gloves on and cleaned the belt with petrol. For a moment I tried to convince myself that this would be enough, but another look at the road ahead made me face the truth and I rummaged in one of the toolboxes for the small screwdriver which I use for link-removal. The toolbox was obscured by one of the panniers which hung over it, but I reckoned I could get the tool out without removing them. The vinyl gloves were not helping sensitivity, but I was doing quite well, I thought, crouching down and easing the pannier up with my shoulder while feeling up into the almost invisible toolbox. 'Almost there ... just a fraction more ...' I gave a slight extra nudge with the shoulder and *H* toppled deliberately and unstoppably away from me and over into the ditch. This was not just a matter of lying on her side, ready to be picked up. She was completely inverted, saddle and handlebars in the bottom of the channel, fuel and oil cascading out of various orifices, wheels and stand pointing up at me.

At times like this I apply the motto of an Australian hero of mine, Bill Moyes. He was one of the first hang glider pilots and has led a life of perpetual achievement and excitement. In tricky situations he would exclaim *Do something! Do anything! Don't just do nothing!* So I did something: I wrestled *H* out of the ditch. I have no idea exactly how I achieved this. I know that by most standards *H* is not a heavy machine, but she's not exactly a moped either. I don't remember what parts of the bike I grabbed hold of and I can't imagine where the strength came from, because, since the heart attack, I have broadly followed the advice to avoid heavy

128

lifting. Anyway, within moments *H* was back on firm ground and the correct way up. The handlebars and controls were twisted out of alignment and the horn bracket bent. Streams of oil and fuel stained her tank; earth clogged her levers. *H* did indeed look pretty sad, but a few minutes with a spanner and a rag had her back in shape. As I should have done in the first place, I now removed the panniers completely before finding the screwdriver for belt shortening and all went well. Back on the road again she climbed away and we dodged in and out of the clouds all the way to the top of the Col de la Croix de Fer (2067m/6781ft).

I was glad to stop at the refuge there for a *croque monsieur*, or as a British pub menu would say, a ham'n'cheese toastie and a hot milky coffee in the French style. I normally prefer my coffee black, but somehow up here in the clouds and icy wind, *café au lait* felt as if it would be more warming. Did the trick. There is indeed a cross of iron, mounted on a rather phallic column. Curiously, neither guidebooks nor Wikipedia are very confident about how or when it got there.

A splendid feature of the ride up is the *Barrage de Grand Maison,* an enormous rock and earth dam. When it first comes into view as you ride along the valley side, the appearance is of a vertical face with what looks like a zig-zag footpath clinging to it. As you ride on, the scale and shape of the thing gradually becomes clear. The height is 160m (525ft) and that little footpath is actually a grand road up a slope of around forty five degrees and can accommodate trucks.

I made a mistake descending from the Croix de Fer; I should have read my map more carefully and back-tracked for a few kilometres to turn onto the Col du Glandon, where I could have picked up a very minor road, the D297. It would have taken us directly to La Chambre, which I thought would make a good staging post for our next big climb, the Col de la Madeleine. Instead I carried straight on down the interminable descent to St Jean de Maurienne. There is nothing wrong with the views here and some of the little villages which straggle down the pass are charming; it's just that it seemed to go on and on. Like Modane, thirty or so kilometres to the east, St Jean de Maurienne is quite a transport hub between France and Italy. It is dominated by a big RTZ plant and served by the Autoroute. We found the town tricky to navigate and it was followed by a dreadful quarter of an hour on the busy D1006, before pulling off, with relief, at the *La Chambre* signpost.

H and I had now left the official Route des Grandes Alpes and were to become free-range again. We were a little frazzled by the events of what had turned out to be a slightly epic day. Fortunately, it was all soon put right by the welcome we received in La Chambre.

The little town looked festive, decked out with colourful bunting. *H* and I chugged slowly through, on the lookout for the tourist office or a suitable hotel. You will have worked out by now that we are not after five-star accommodation – we are much more at home in family-run hotels, preferably with that peculiarly French charm which I have known from time to time since the 1950s. They are getting harder to find and one has to accept that one has to take the rough with the smooth. Tonight we were to drop lucky and our choice turned out to be lovely and smooth. I parked by a couple of other bikes at a likely looking spot in the centre and was immediately hailed by a small group of motorcyclists at a pavement cafe. "I can't stop", I explained, "I have to find a hotel."

"The hotel is here!" They indicated a *Hotel Bristol* sign I had not noticed a few metres away. "But it does not open for another half-hour. Come and join us." By now the afternoon was gone and evening was upon us. I was quite anxious to find a bed, but they were insistent. "You'll get in there, for sure." I was told, and an extra chair was drawn up to the table. "You are English?" ... it was more of a statement than a question. I would like to think that they had worked this out from the GB plate on *H*'s rear mudguard, but in truth my accent is a dead giveaway. "What would you like to drink? Beer? Coffee? Tea?" Following a lifetime of disappointment I normally avoid tea anywhere beyond the borders of Yorkshire, but now, after the adventures of the day I was in a gambling mood: "I would love a cup of tea, s'il vous plaît."

My hosts were from the Pyrenees, making a motorcycle camping tour of the Alps, for a change. They were very enthusiastic about all types of motorcycling and took an immediate shine to *H*. Almost everyone I met on my European tours seemed to grasp what I was doing and accept the motivation easily. Soon my drink arrived in the form of a fine white pot full of builder's tea; no room for complaint there! The cafe behind our table was a classic-motorcycle themed establishment, packed with exhibits and posters and even a complete '50s bike screwed to the wall above the stairs. They were just getting ready to close, but generously gave me a guided tour first.

Inside the chaotic motorcycle café

The half-hour passed effortlessly and eventually we took our leave and looked forward to possibly meeting in the morning somewhere on the Col de la Madeleine. I strolled into the hotel and was given a room with a view straight up the road to the Col.

Approx 100 miles/160Km

Chapter 18

The baggage chronicles

The problem of what to take with you on a long journey on a slow bike, or come to think of it, almost any journey on any bike, is one that has to be faced early on. Preferably before setting out. My thoughts are relevant to sissies like me who intend to find roofed overnight accommodation – with en-suite facilities whenever possible. Those heroes going motorcycle camping, which is a whole different discipline involving kitchen sinks and spades for digging latrines, are another species altogether and should seek guidance elsewhere. After the first trip, they will either vow 'never again', or will persist and get good at it. I hope some will write books about it. At 75 I'm not going to try. I offer the following hints and tips in the devout hope that others may learn from my errors, so here goes:

On my End-to-End ride I used soft rectangular throw-over panniers made for use by pedal cyclists. They worked well and remained dry, but this year I intended to tour more and invested in a pair specifically designed for the motorcyclist. There was nothing wrong with them and their elasticised yellow rain covers had been put to the test repeatedly during my wet ride in June. They passed. However, they were of a more streamlined shape than the cycle ones and turned out to be slightly less practical. They were slung either side of the carrier and took my clothing and personal gear. Clothes and sponge-bag went in one side; books, maps, diary and sundries in the other. Motorcycle spares and tools were kept in a leather doctor's-type bag strapped down onto the carrier.

Less is good

Assuming you are not going to the Antarctic or the fringes of civilization, you will be able to purchase almost anything you may have forgotten in the way of clothing, toiletries etc. as you go along – and often for less than at home. After all, the locals manage, don't they? A tube of *Rai* clothes-washing gel, or similar, will mean you can get away with just one extra tee-shirt and pair of underpants. Usually such things will dry overnight and if the worst comes to the worst, a couple of consecutive days of pants-wearing rarely lead to fatality.

A good sweater is an essential. The one which went with me is a cashmere, bought from TKMaxx for just the price of a normal woolly elsewhere. Problem is that you have to do a lot of sorting-through of their rails before you come up with anything decent, and even then there is no guarantee you'll find it. Persistence pays, but be prepared to work on the princess/frog kissing principle. Cashmere is great because it packs a lot of warmth into a small space. Apart from that, I carried a pair of cotton trousers, two pairs of socks and a pair of lightweight deck shoes. I allowed myself the extravagance of one extra long-sleeved T-shirt, underpants, and that was about it. I think I could manage to make myself look superficially passable when entering hotel dining rooms in the evening, so nothing else mattered really.

As well as the bags mentioned above, I had an elastic cargo net of the type designed for motorcyclists, and a small plastic tarpaulin. The cargo net is a versatile creature: by day it clamped my folded-up long waterproof coat on top of everything else on the carrier. By night, if *H* had to sleep in the open, it was used to hook the edges of the tarp together underneath the bike to keep the weather off.

Money

There is no shortage of roadside petrol pumps in France, but they are usually un-manned and you need to have a cash card of a type you can rely on. Don't assume that your UK credit card will always work. Quite often it won't in a surprising number of European countries. Also, increasingly, if you haven't informed your card company that you are going to be abroad it may be rejected by the card company's security software. Moreover, the charges for buying a few litres of fuel on a Sterling card can be disproportionate. None of this is a problem if you take a Euro cash card with you. I get mine from Thomas Cook and they have always worked perfectly for me. Admittedly, they have to be loaded up with funds in advance, but that seems to be the only drawback. Beats travellers' cheques and cash hands down!

Tools and equipment

I have gradually managed to trim down the number of tools and spares I carry. When I started doing longish jaunts on ancient bikes, I used to load up with a complete set of spanners and every spare part I could think of. Now it is a lot less.

(Note to non-technical readers: *you are free to skip this lot. There is no compulsory test at the end of the book*)

I take two top-quality adjustable spanners. The smaller one lives in my jacket pocket so it's readily to hand for quick adjustments such as nipping up control levers. There's no escaping the fact that these simple old bikes do vibrate a bit, so things loosen up occasionally. *H*'s vibrations are of low frequency and don't numb my fingers the way my 1950sTriumph Tiger 100 used to. The larger adjustable has been customised to the extent of cutting an inch or so off the handle so that it will fit into one of *H*'s side toolboxes. Apart from these, I have a few special spanners for such tasks as removing the valve caps in the cylinder head, dismantling the carburettor and adjusting wheel bearings. And, of course, little ones for the magneto. I don't bother with feeler gauges because I find my thumbnail is about right for the spark-plug gap and a piece of paper will do for magneto points.

I allow myself the luxury of three screwdrivers: one large-ish and one small, for use on routine screw-driving duties. The third is a very old, worn-smooth item which is useless when confronted with a screw but is ideal for extracting links from the drive belt.

A small Mole-type grip has often come in handy. I never have a job in mind for it when setting out, but invariably I have had cause to bless it at some time on a trip.

That's about it for tools except for the trump card: a Leatherman! There's nothing better for old-time riders to carry with them. In case you have never heard of such a thing, it is a multi-tool which is made in the USA. It has much in common with a Swiss Army knife, but with more emphasis on the plier/screwdriver capability. There are a few models to choose from and mine is called the *Wave*. It combines wire-cutting pliers with file, knife, saws, scissors, screwdrivers and bottle-opener in one tool, and it all works! So often combinations are 90% useless, but I think the Leatherman is 100% use*ful*. Not only is the design ingenious and practical, everything about it is top quality. The only make I have seen which comes anywhere near is Gerber. My Leatherman has been used and abused for many years now and still feels like new. There are now many imitations at a fraction of the price, but in my experience there is no clearer illustration of the old saying that 'you get what you pay for'.

Spares

I packed a spare valve and valve-spring for the engine. There was a spare set of points for the magneto and a float for the carburettor. An extra clutch cable is permanently taped in place on the bike all the time. Some cable ties, the solderless nipple for cable repairs, a roll of insulating tape and a spare inner tube completed my spares kit. I used only the nipple and a couple of cable ties.

Clothing

I always find it hard to decide what to wear for my journeys. *H* and I move very slowly so we don't need modern motorcycle gear suited to 100 mph cruising. On the other hand, when it rains we get just as wet as anyone else. On the optimistic assumption that September in France would be warm, I decided to wear what I use for summer rallies in Britain. This consists of an Irish thornproof tweed jacket and waistcoat which was once part of my best suit, tailor-made for me forty years ago. These go above a pair of moleskin walking breeches which I have had almost as long. Woollen socks, leather boots and thin gloves finished it all off except for the head. Again, banking on clement weather, I chanced using an aged pudding-basin crash helmet as I find modern ones far too warm unless it really is freezing.

In case of rain, I carried the Australian drover's coat which is fine at modest speeds. It is made of waxed cotton and has acquired lots of character in the ten years or so that I have used it. It has also lost some of its water-resistant capability, but doesn't do badly. Like its relative, the Barbour suit, it has an uncanny ability to transfer disproportionate amounts of grime onto the collar and cuffs of any shirt worn anywhere near it.

As it turned out, this rather quaint outfit served well. I find the extra pockets provided by the jacket/waistcoat combination are a blessing on a journey like mine. It was coolish when the weather was hot and just about warm enough when it was not. The only thing I missed was a pair of warmer gloves for use on the high passes.

Electronic equipment

I set out with an iPad and an iPhone. In a mild frenzy of cutting out anything I thought I could manage without, I left the iPad in the van, something I later regretted when I got short of reading matter. The iPhone is a wonderful piece of equipment which can apparently play all the better-known hymns and produce rabbits from hats in the hands of any intelligent nine-year-old, but that rules me out. I can, however, use it pretty fluently as a telephone and text machine, and I did. The problems start when it comes to hooking it up to the internet because I have read so many horror stories about innocents like me who have left them switched on while abroad and ended up with a phone bill about level with the Greek national debt, that I never dare activate the 'roaming' facility. I wonder what I really missed? The weather forecast app (I have to grit my teeth to type that) would have been handy occasionally, but I could usually get enough info from TV in the hotels. The GPS is one of those things which would apparently be perfect on a ride like mine, but a paper map is better because its scale doesn't keep changing and its batteries never run out.

I will admit to a basic error of judgement where the camera was concerned. I have a small Panasonic Lumix which looks like a camera and behaves exactly as one should. Put it in the most inexperienced hands and it will produce perfect results at once. It fits easily in a pocket, but such was my determination to keep packing to a minimum, I decided to leave it in the van and rely on my iPhone for all photographic duties. Serious error. Although the iPhone takes acceptable images provided you keep within its limitations and don't get too ambitious, it doesn't look like a camera and doesn't handle like one. There is nothing instinctive about it. Consequently, when I gave it to bystanders with the request to take a photo of me and *H* together at beauty spots, the bystanders usually managed to take an out-of-focus shot of their own forefingers. The really clumsy ones got their thumbs in too. The few that avoided that error usually managed accidently to switch to the *video* mode, which is equally useless for reproduction purposes.

Tyres

In contrast to the Buck Rogers' capabilities of the iPhone, the tyres that *H* rides on are of a type that hasn't been used on new motorcycles for almost ninety years. They serve well enough, but are very different to modern ones and need knowing!

A mystique has built up around the *beaded-edge* tyres of the early vintage years, but they are really simple to understand and usually quite easy to fit. Those on my Triumph are typical of its period; beaded-edge tyres moulded from rubber with an inner layer of canvas reinforcement. There are no wires around the bead; instead the inward-curved edges of the wheel rim engage with deep grooves moulded into the tyre casing. The inner tube is completely contained within the casing and is prevented from touching the ends of the spokes by continuous flaps which are also part of the cover – no need for the rim tapes which are essential with wired-edge tyres on spoked rims.

The picture below is worth a thousand words.

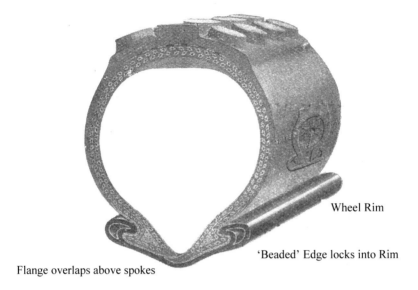

Wheel Rim

'Beaded' Edge locks into Rim

Flange overlaps above spokes

Image of cross section of tyre

Due to the way the cover encloses the tube, the fitting process may seem curious to anyone familiar only with more modern types. The trick is to start with the tyre right off the rim. The core is fitted into the valve and the inner tube then inflated until it will just – but only just – hold its shape. It is then wangled into the cover, making sure that the valve emerges exactly at the point where the flaps have been cut away to leave a hole for it. (If you are fitting a new cover, you have had to cut this hole yourself, using a very sharp knife.)

Now the tyre is offered up to the wheel and the valve slipped through its hole in the rim. At this stage I find it useful to screw the cap on loosely to prevent the valve accidentally slipping out during the imminent mild wrestling bout. Then, starting near to the valve, which you need to be pushing up into the cover from time-to-time to reassure yourself that it is not trapped, guide the beads into the rim with fingers and thumb. The task will often look hopeless at first, but with a bit of effort and patience it will all go together. It is often possible to do all this without using tyre levers, although with a brand-new cover you may have to resort to them. If possible, do not use any lubricant as it can encourage the tyre to 'creep' on the rim when on the road. That can be severe enough to pull the valve out and leave you with a wrecked tube.

Attempting to fit one side of the cover to the rim before putting the tube in is doomed to failure, as is trying to fit a completely flat tube – it needs just a few puffs of air in it to minimise the chance of it becoming nipped during the fitting process.

In service, I like to keep at least 40psi (2.8 bar) in the tyres to ensure that they do not move on the rim. I also prefer not to screw the locking nut on the valve down tight, so that any movement can be easily spotted by the valve beginning to slope relative to the rim.

These beaded-edge type tyres persisted up to the late 1920s and I am not sure exactly why. I suspect that patent protection may have had something to do with it as the wired-edge type, so apparently superior, was in use on bicycles from the 1890s. Or it may simply be that the technology of bonding wire into rubber could cope with bike loads but was not sufficiently developed to resist harder use on motorcycles and cars. In practice a beaded-edger is more eager to leave the rim after a rapid deflation than is its wired counterpart. I have experienced this a couple of times and it does concentrate the mind greatly during the deceleration process.

Veteran and vintage riders were always prepared for punctures and much more philosophical about the inconvenience than we have become: they had to be, for they were riding on unmade roads liberally scattered with horseshoe and boot nails, and rubber technology was in its infancy.

I always carry a spare tube with me, as well as a small bicycle type repair outfit with patches. I have no faith whatever in 'instant-seal-and-inflate' devices, which I am sure are worthwhile if you are just out for a day on a modern bike with tubeless tyres, but I can't imagine them working their magic on an inner-tube with a two-inch split in it. If I am going to have to fit a patch or new tube sooner or later, I would rather do it to a tyre free of leaked sticky goo.

As I write, beaded-edge tyres are available in a limited number of sizes and generally they perform well, but are usually black. In the years up to and including the Great War, motor tyres were made from natural rubber and would have been white, or, more accurately a pale creamy grey. This was not a matter of style or show, but because the technique of adding carbon-black was not discovered until around 1910, by B F Goodrich in the USA. The carbon greatly increased durability of tyres, but it took quite a few more years for it to become generally adopted. When I first heard this I was a little sceptical, but the more I looked at contemporary photos of pioneer bikes and cars, right up to the mid1920s, the more I became convinced. It also explains why the Michelin Man is white!

Chapter 19

The final Cols

Thursday September 20

I liked La Chambre, even though it is severely over-supplied in the church bell department. I was woken at seven a.m. by a rather flat one which struck eight-and-a-bit. The bit was a sort of half-clang, as if the ringer had tried to stop in time but not quite managed it. The performance was OK for waking you up, but rather lacking for time-check purposes. As I lay in bed contemplating breakfast, a different bell started up and I counted the rings to see if this rival establishment could manage a bit more precision. Well, it comfortably overshot the seven-clang mark and continued non-stop to eighty-three. If that didn't get the faithful out to pray, I suspect nothing would.

I am not a great fan of church bells and my home is mercifully out of range of any. It is not, however, out of range of the BBC which frequently irritates me early on Sunday mornings when I have just woken and made the mistake of switching on Radio 4. Typically, I will be enjoying an extra few minutes lie-in before getting *H* ready for a day out at an eagerly anticipated vintage event, when my senses are assaulted by their *Bells on Sunday* feature. This consists of nothing else for minutes on end. To me it always sounds like a junkyard falling over a cliff. I do not claim to be musical.

I particularly liked the view from my hotel room. It overlooked the start of the road out of town leading to my final climbs. The junction was decorated with bright coloured bunting on which the flags were not the normal triangles, but more like little T-shirts. Eventually the penny dropped and I realised that the Tour de France had passed through a few weeks earlier and the flags represented *maillots* in the colours of the various leaders. (Photo page 133)

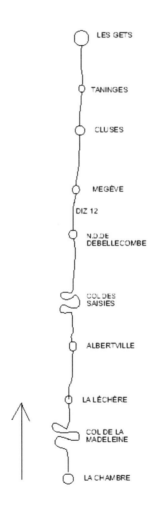

Throughout my ride I kept being reminded of the Tour, usually by graffiti on the roads themselves, and developed an ever-stronger feeling of respect for the participants in that brutal discipline.

Yesterday had been good for my confidence as the repaired rim was standing up well to the hard work I had asked of it. I checked the route on my map and the D 213 to the Col de la Madeleine (1993m/6539ft) looked decidedly more in the 'minor road' category than some of the other cols and I wondered what I was in for. I was away quite early and the climbing started immediately. I had the road to myself virtually all the way and felt very much on my own. Towards the top, in that level of a mountain which really does feel like the middle of nowhere, there was a lot of heavy-duty road repair going on and I got waves and even a cheer or two from the gang. It was bitterly cold and I could have done with lined gloves, but the perpetually changing mountain panorama gave me plenty of other things to think about. My road was clear, but there was lots of fresh snow away to the north on the Mont Blanc Massif.

As expected, the Madeleine was a tough climb with some wonderful sequences of hairpins. The mountain ascents on the Tour de France are categorised from *Fourth* (short and just steep enough to make you suffer) up to *First* (long and utterly punishing). They qualify for 'King of the Mountain' points accordingly. However, the Madeleine is beyond any of these and is classified *Hors Catégorie* (HC) which are the worst of the lot. *Indescribable* would be a fair free translation! I used bottom gear much more often than usual, but by 10.15 we were over the top. The signboard reads *2000m* – it somehow grew an extra seven metres in time for the 2012 Tour! Regardless of the height, it really is a bugger of a road which I thoroughly enjoyed tackling successfully!

Of course, the climb was followed by the inevitable descent, in this case to the valley of the Isère, much of it through occasionally wooded pastures. I loved it all and stayed on minor roads to cross the river at St Paul. Then onwards, keeping the Isère on my left shoulder as we took the back road to Albertville, where I refuelled with the usual lack of drama thanks to my Eurocard. Here we turned right for Les Saisies, which put us back on to the official Route des Grandes Alpes again.

The Col des Saisies was as tough from the south as it had been from the north almost a couple of weeks ago on our way down. Not a great problem after so much practice, but none of the *Route* is just a formality. I cannot remember exactly how many days I have been riding, but it simply doesn't matter: everyone has been good and every one a small adventure. When you can say that in your mid 70s, it is hard to ask for more. The roads begin to feel increasingly familiar and my navigation becomes even more casual than usual, with the result that I take a wrong turning after Notre Dame de Bellecombe. I realise the error when we enter the outskirts of Megeve. At the last moment I spot a convenient entrance to an upward-sloping car park on the right and we swoop in and roll to what an uninformed observer would have assumed was a beautifully judged arrival. Little would they realise the degree of brakelessness we were experiencing.

A few minutes with the map and I decide to cheat and carry on up the D1212 which leads straight to Cluses, rather than slavishly follow the *Route* via Le Grand Bornand and its associated Cols, the Aravis and Colombière which we had ridden on the way out. Works out fine. The D1212 is busy, but not hectic and we get to

Cluses with minimum drama. We park there for a swift coffee, watching the traffic and feeling pretty satisfied, but the stop is short because Les Gets and the van are within easy reach. I hardly dare look at the rear rim for fear that I will find it on the point of disintegration, but a quick waggle at it suggests that it is still bearing up well. Curiously, now that it has been on *H* for a couple of hard days it seems to have blended in and doesn't look quite so outrageously patched-up any more. There is a simple explanation for this: I am getting used to it ...

Now there is simply the village of Tangines and the climb up the Gorge to Les Gets. All rather main-roadish, but *H* runs as sweetly as ever all the way to the hotel *A La Bonne Franquette* where my VW van is still waiting, shaded under its tree.

Finished with engines. I turn off the petrol cock and allow *H* to tick over gently and consume the fuel remaining in the carburettor, before removing the baggage and wheeling her up the ramp into the van. The quiet is lovely. There is no sign of activity at the hotel, but I find a chair and stretch out for a few minutes in the sunlight. It was a small achievement in the overall size of life, but, oh, it does feel good! Perhaps this is what it was all for – a superb feeling of completeness; a task finished, a dream fulfilled.

H tucked away again, and the cheerful owners of A La Bonne Franquette

Approx 90 miles/145km

Chapter 20

Fancy joining in?

I ride *H* in any suitable events I can find. I have a couple of other machines which I can use, one older, one much younger, but I prefer to use *H* if I can. We will tackle anything except speed events and enjoy being part of the vintage motorcycle scene in Britain and abroad. A feature of the activity is that a motorcycle doesn't have to be terribly old to take part – any machine aged 25 years or more can come under the umbrella of the Vintage Motor Cycle Club (VMCC) which is the main UK organisation. However, that is just the starting point. Obviously an event which will suit a fast bike from the 1980s will not do for those which may be 100 years old or even more; here's a run-down on the main classes and categories for touring bikes as are generally recognised in Britain:

Veteran
Motorcycles manufactured before 1 January 1915. Within this group is a subdivision for those built before 1908; they are often referred to as *Pioneer* machines.

Vintage
1915 to 1930 inclusive.

Post Vintage
1931 to 1941

Classic
Older than 25 years

I can't summarise accurately the attraction of riding machines as old as *H* and I certainly couldn't justify it to a rationalist. It is a blend of many influences: there is the spare functionality of the machine which has an attraction in times of ever-increasing complexity in the gadgets of everyday life. There is satisfaction in simply keeping her running well. There is even pleasure in the smell of old oil and slightly stale petrol when I enter the garage. I don't know why my taste directs me towards having an extra affection for belt-drivers – which were completely obsolete by the time I started motorcycling in the '50s. It's not normal! Most of the old-bike enthusiasts from my generation lean towards riding the road-burners of the '50s and '60s which they gazed at in showroom windows when they were new, but were beyond their pockets. Beauties such as the ubiquitous Triumph Bonneville, the Vincent Black Shadow and the Gold Star BSAs. I like them, but wouldn't swap *H* for one. Others seek out commuting curiosities, which in my book would include the LE Velocette, the police 'Noddy Bike' of the 1950s, or the NSU Quickly which would have shown the British industry how to build a decent moped if the management hadn't all been looking the other way. Now we also see a huge growth of interest in older Japanese bikes too. None of this matters: the basic pleasure is the same regardless of whether the object of one's attention originated in Birmingham or Hamamatsu.

Now what?

If you think that you might enjoy being involved in any part of the old motorcycle scene, *join a club*! As I mentioned, the VMCC caters for all makes and all ages and is divided into more than seventy regional sections, so there is bound to be one near you.

If your tastes are focused on a particular make, there are also many one-make clubs which are not hard to find out about through the internet. And don't imagine that you need an expensive thoroughbred to enjoy the fun: one of the most active and innovative associations is the National Autocycle and Cyclemotor Club (NACC). So whether you want to race an '80s Kawasaki, potter along on a Minimotor or coax a 100-year-old belt-driven relic over mountains, there will be a club out there to suit.

I strongly recommend finding the club before investing in a bike, as clubs are an excellent source of intelligence through which you can learn what machines are likely to be available, which to avoid, what you may expect to pay and who is fair to deal with. Although old motorcycles of every type have appreciated in value, even through the recession, it is still easy to get your fingers burnt when buying one. If you just want one to look at and occasionally polish, then it won't matter to you if the bearings are worn out. However, if you are like me and get most of the pleasure out of bringing the bike to life and riding it quite a lot, then you must expect to spend a fair amount on mechanical fettling before relying on it for any distance. It is a sad reflection that not all the machines which look great are sound underneath. There are also plenty of forgeries. That's not as dramatic as it sounds, but the newcomer needs to know the sort of thing that goes on. For example, not everything that looks like a Triumph Bonneville left the factory as one. Just changing a few components on a Speed Twin and a good repaint can look pretty convincing to someone who is desperate to find a Bonnie. Buyer beware!

Typical club events for road bikes are usually fairly informal and consist of a run around a route set out on minor roads. Route cards are often provided and a 'sweeper' vehicle will follow the last runners to make sure everyone gets home in the event of a breakdown. It is all very casual and there is no time schedule to follow. The socialising before and after the ride is as important as the ride itself. A few of the runs have a timed element, requiring an average speed to be maintained. I used to enjoy these, but since I started in the 1960s, the law has become much more restrictive concerning any kind of rally timing on public roads. Consequently they are difficult to organise and marshal and are now very hard to find. The VMCC's Banbury Run is one of the last.

Many enthusiasts get great pleasure out of preparing their motorcycles to 'concours condition' and keeping them that way. The aim is for the bike to be spotless and correct in the smallest detail. A good one will look just as if it has rolled off the stand at a long-past motorcycle show at Olympia or Earl's Court. I am secretly rather jealous of those who have the time and patience to achieve this and I acknowledge that I will never enter their ranks. I am happy with the 'fairly clean and serviceable' look. At the other end of the spectrum are those who prize originality above all else and like to use the bikes in as near the 'as-found' state as possible. I believe the French may have been in at the beginning of this movement and the expression 'trouvé dans son jus' – literally *found in its own gravy* – has come to be widely used. I am all for a bit of authentic patina, but it can be overdone: I once watched the frame of an ancient but recently discovered Peugeot separate into halves under the influence of its patina when it was proudly ridden on its first public appearance.

Prestige events

Apart from activities at local club level, there are a few national events which act as focal points for thousands of enthusiasts, either as riders or spectators. The British season tends to start with the Pioneer Run© which is organised by the Sunbeam Motor Cycle Club Ltd each March. The route starts at Tattenham Corner on Epsom racecourse and finishes at Brighton, and only bikes built before 1915 may take part. Even with that restriction, almost 400 machines enter each year. This is the place to see the earliest historic rarities in action!

The VMCC's Banbury Run takes place in mid-June and is currently based at the Heritage Motor Centre at Gaydon, Warwickshire. This is limited to pre-1931 machines and brings together the largest concentration of genuine Vintage and Veteran bikes in the world. In spite of having a limit of 600, the Banbury is always over-subscribed and one needs to get the entry form in several months early.

Everything else

I have mentioned only the sort of road events which I like to ride in. The old-motorcycle scene is almost infinitely diverse and there are clubs for everything, whether it is historic racing, sprinting or the arcane peculiarities of long out-of-production makes. There are huge shows which incorporate autojumbles, such as those at Stafford and Stanford Hall. And interest in old motorcycles is not confined to Britain by any means. I ride frequently in Belgium and Germany and it is only lack of time and money which has kept me away from many other European countries, or indeed, much of the rest of the world ...

NW 10/06/2013

Some more reading

Books in English about the Route des Grandes Alpes do not seem to exist, although there is a lot of helpful stuff on the Internet. For those with school French I suggest:

Les Alpes à moto ISBN 978-2-06-715547-3 Published by Michelin, 2011 The maps are particularly useful

La Route des Grandes Alpes ISBN 978-2-7373-5623-0 Author Phillippe Lemonnier Published by Éditions Ouest-France, 2012 Nice photos and straightforward narrative. Easy to follow.

Other long rides

By the standards of heroic round-the-world bike riders my runs are no more than afternoon diversions. All I can claim in common is the urge to write a book about it. I enjoy reading other riders' travellers' tales, some much more than others. Here are four of my all-time favourites. Digest this lot and I believe you will get a better picture of the world and the changes in it than any history book will reveal:

Round the World on a Wheel by John Foster Fraser, published by Thomas Nelson and Sons, 1898. Fraser was a well-connected aristocrat who, with two similarly mounted companions, rode right around the world on Rover bicycles towards the end of Victoria's reign. It must have been amazingly tough, but Fraser narrates it all in a gung-ho Bulldog Drummond style which makes light of surviving smallpox and shooting the occasional dog with the revolver he kept to hand. In so doing he also exposes a condescension to other nations and peoples which both built the Empire and made its collapse inevitable.

The original is long out of print, but copies are easily available.

One-man Caravan by Robert Edison Fulton Jr. My edition was published by the Travel Book Club, London ca 1938.

A well-written tale of a lone ride home from England to the USA via almost everywhere else during the 1930s. His machine was a 600cc Douglas which was prepared for him at the factory. An easy read.

India The Shimmering Dream by Max Reisch, originally published in German in the 1930s, this edition was translated by Alison Falls in 2010. ISBN 978-0-9556595-9-1
Panther Publishing, High Wycombe.

A great tale of two Austrian students who, in 1933, became the first motorcyclists to ride from Vienna to India, taking in much of North Africa on the way. Their transport was a 6hp Puch two-stroke which performed brilliantly in spite of being severely overloaded from day one. Alison Falls' translation is superb and it is hard to believe that any of the flavour of the author's original German text has been lost.

Investment Biker by Jim Rogers 1994 ISBN 0-471-96126-4
John Wiley and Sons, Chichester

I suspect that it is not easy to imagine an outrageously wealthy hedge fund manager that you would really like to spend time with, but Jim Rogers comes across as such a man. Just after the Berlin Wall collapsed, Jim and his companion Tabitha made a grand world tour on a brace of BMWs. They had the resources to stay in the best hotels and did so whenever possible. Why not if you've got the cash? But Jim is also a brilliant observer, not just of the passing scene, but also of the disintegrating communist world and the emergence of Far Eastern economies. He also has a sharp eye for investment opportunities. This book is a great way to learn about economics, markets and geography without realising you are doing it. Reading his words again almost twenty years later shows his assessments to have been pretty well spot-on. I guess you don't get to be a multi-millionaire just by accident! Highly recommended.

This has been my personal selection of long-ride books. I have re-read them all while writing of my Alpine run. They span more than a century. Some big names are missing; usually because I found them a bit dull and repetitive or I felt they took themselves a bit too seriously. I like my rider/writers to have a hint of the nutter coming to the surface now and then!

Noel Whittall